Connecting Content and Language
for English Language Learners

Author
Eugenia Mora-Flores, Ed.D.
Foreword
Lindsey M. Guccione

 SHELL EDUCATION

Publishing Credits

Dona Herweck Rice, *Editor-in-Chief*; Lee Aucoin, *Creative Director*;
Don Tran, *Print Production Manager;* Timothy J. Bradley, *Illustration Manager*;
Conni Medina, M.A.Ed., *Editorial Director*; Evelyn Garcia, *Associate Education Editor*;
Juan Chavolla, *Interior Layout Designer;* Corinne Burton, M.A.Ed., *Publisher*

Shell Education

5301 Oceanus Drive
Huntington Beach, CA 92649-1030
http://www.shelleducation.com
ISBN 978-1-4258-0800-6
© 2011 Shell Educational Publishing, Inc.
Reprinted 2013

Table of Contents

Foreword. 07

Acknowledgements 09

Introduction 11

Chapter 1: Guiding Principles 17

    My Journey as a Bilingual Child. 17

    My Experiences as a Teacher
       of English Language Learners 18

    Reinventing Myself as a Teacher for
       English-Only Settings. 24

    Reflection Questions. 26

Chapter 2: Language Development 27

    Language Acquisition 27

    Language Transfer. 28

    Learning a Language. 31

    Learning a Second Language 33

    Language Development Levels. 37

    Conclusion 40

    Reflection Questions. 41

Chapter 3: Academic Language. 43

    Vocabulary. 44

    Functions and Forms of Language 46

    Academic Language Development 47

Language Input. 48

Specially Designed Academic Instruction in English 49

    Anticipation Guides. 49

    Carousel 51

    Jigsaw 51

    Multimedia Presentations. 52

Academic Language Output. 53

Facilitating Thinking. 55

Conclusion 58

Reflection Questions. 59

Chapter 4: Creating a Language-Rich Environment. 61

Building a Classroom Community (Physical Space). 63

Peer-to-Peer Interaction 64

Teacher as Listener 67

Low Risk, High Success Contexts 70

Interactive Read-Alouds 72

Daily Shared-Reading Opportunities 73

Words Introduced Orally and in Context. 74

Abundant Classroom Library 77

Explicit Language Environment 78

Conclusion 79

Reflection Questions. 80

Chapter 5: Literacy Instruction for
English Language Learners: Essential Elements 81

Cognates 83

Letter-Sound Connections 85

Developing Oral Language 86

Strategies for Developing Oral Language 87

    Student-Teacher Talk 87

    Pair-Share 87

    Table Talk 90

    Find Someone Who 91

Phonemic Awareness and Phonics 93

Strategies for Teaching Phonics 94

    Word Building 94

    Word Families 94

    Letter-Sound Collage 95

    Phonics Carousel 97

Vocabulary Instruction 98

Strategies for Teaching Vocabulary 99

    Vocabulary Self-Selection 100

    Where in the World? 101

    Morphology 101

Written Discourse 103

Scaffolding Writing 107

Reading and Writing Connections 112

Authentic Writing Opportunities 113

Strategies for Teaching Reading Comprehension 113

    Sticky Notes 114

    Reflective Journals 115

    Inquiry Charts 115

Survey, Question, Predict, Read, Recite, Review
   (SQPRRR/SQP3R) 116

Student Investment 118

Motivation 119

Conclusion 120

Reflection Questions 121

**Chapter 6: Developing Language
   Across the Curriculum** 123

English Language Development 124

Strategies for Teaching ELD 127

   Tea Party 128

   Travelers and Talkers 129

   Lines of Communication 131

   World in a Bag 133

   Four-Corner Literature Review 135

Content ELD 136

Academic Language Development
   and Content ELD 140

Conclusion 141

Reflection Questions 142

Concluding Thoughts 143

Appendices 145

Appendix A: Cognates 145

Appendix B: Language Functions and Forms 152

Appendix C: Glossary 158

References 161

Foreword

Connecting Content and Language for English Language Learners provides teachers with a practical resource for incorporating effective language instruction throughout the school day. The number of English language learners has increased immensely over the past 15 years. In the decade between 1995 and 2005, the number of English language learners in K–12 schools grew to more than five million, with some states growing as much as 200 percent (OELA 2007). Teachers today must be equipped with strategies to support the linguistic and cultural needs of their diverse classrooms. Eugenia Mora-Flores does just that in *Connecting Content and Language for English Language Learners* by sharing her experiences and providing concrete and research-based instructional ideas that teachers will be able to implement in their classrooms the following day.

All students deserve a rich and rigorous learning environment and educational experience. Eugenia Mora-Flores draws on her experience as a bilingual student, classroom teacher, literacy coach, professor and professional developer to empower classroom teachers to challenge and engage each student as a novice, apprentice, and expert as they move through their language and educational journey. *Connecting Content and Language for English Language Learners* includes specific strategies, methods, instructional approaches, resources, activities and reflective questions to assist teachers in their quest to provide comprehensible input and assist their students in a successful educational experience.

With a focus on helping teachers create authentic interactions for students to think, talk, and respond, Eugenia Mora-Flores draws on the research literature *and* classroom experiences. Each chapter includes Classroom Connections where she shares stories connecting the concepts to actual classroom settings. The Reflection Questions at the end of each chapter invite readers to reflect on their experiences, as well as the pedagogical implications of the text.

Eugenia Mora-Flores grounds the text with guiding principles she has learned from working with English language learners in many grades with diverse curricular demands. Regardless of the demands or type of required instruction (bilingual, English immersion, etc.), she emphasizes the vital role that understanding the process of learning a second language can play in helping teachers facilitate language development. She highlights the importance of creating a language rich-environment with effective literacy instruction, which assists in the acquisition of academic language necessary for English language learners to become successful in school. Eugenia Mora-Flores provides classroom stories, detailed ideas, and photographs to help support readers in understanding not only the value but also the practical "how to" aspects of creating it. *Connecting Content and Language for English Language Learners* helps educators realize that with high expectations and thoughtful instruction, English language learners are capable of high levels of academic achievement. Eugenia Mora-Flores takes a compelling stance as she celebrates the work of teachers of English language learners and reminds us that our work with these students will empower them for a lifetime.

—Lindsey M. Guccione
Assistant Professor of Early Childhood Education
School of Teacher Education
University of Northern Colorado

Acknowledgements

This book came together because of the hard work and dedication of many educators working with English language learners. Angelica and Leo Machado, as always, you have welcomed me into your classrooms and shared the amazing things you are doing with your students. Your passion for teaching is apparent in the success of your students and their desire to learn. Mr. Baumann, you have always supported my work and believed in me as a teacher and as a teacher educator. Thank you for always opening the doors to your school.

To all the teachers with whom I have had the pleasure of working, I have learned so much from you and your work with English language learners. Together I believe we have done some wonderful things for children. I truly believe that we can continue to learn and contribute to the future success of this growing student population.

Conni Medina, thank you for believing in me. Your support has been inspiring and has fueled my passion for writing. Evelyn Garcia, thank you for helping me strengthen the book and pushing me to stretch my thinking.

Having the time to write and complete the book was only possible because of my husband, Rudy, and my three amazing children, Emilia, Aidan, and Samantha. You have been patient with me when I needed to write, and you kept me going when I wanted to take a break. Thank you for welcoming me after a long day of writing with open arms and smiling faces.

To my parents, I thank you for sharing the gift of language. Growing up bilingual and understanding what it means to learn a language has inspired my work with English language learners.

Introduction

My goal in writing this book is to empower teachers to believe in their students and themselves as teachers of English language learners. We often lack a sense of self-confidence when we encounter challenges in our profession. We can feel frustrated and ineffective when we see our students staring back at us in puzzlement. We think about our preparation as teachers, trying to remember what we learned about English language learners and how to support them. Unfortunately, most teacher preparation programs do not prepare teachers well for working with English language learners (Lucas, Villegas, and Freedson-Gonzalez 2008). With a lack of preparation, we find ourselves reverting back to traditional pedagogical approaches that do not work with English language learners. We talk *at* students and have them complete worksheets where they just fill in the blank or copy the answer from the board. We overwhelm them with language and content without taking time to check for understanding.

I can remember what it was like from year to year when a new group of students entered the room ready to learn. It was my responsibility to provide them with a quality and holistic education in which they had opportunities to explore content, engage with literature and their peers, and demonstrate their learning in a variety of ways. Yet daily, I found myself questioning my approaches and asking myself, "Are my students learning?" I began to think about what it means to learn a new language and learn *in* a new language at the same time. In my own struggles I began to feel empowered. I had the potential to do something great—the power to help my English language learners navigate this difficult task and learn alongside them. I came to understand that every task had its challenges, but with every challenge came success and an amazing learning opportunity. Though this was my journey, I also began to realize that I was not alone. Many teachers struggle when faced with the challenges of working with English language learners.

I vividly remember a comment I heard from a teacher working with English language learners that struck me and made me realize how powerless we can feel in our work as teachers. I had been teaching language arts methods to pre-service teachers at a large university located in a diverse urban area. As part of my class, the students were required to complete fieldwork in the local district around campus. During a class discussion, one of my students shared a comment made by her master teacher. The master teacher was the certified classroom teacher in the field to which my student teacher was assigned. The master teacher had said, "Don't worry about doing anything different with these kids [English language learners], they can't understand you anyway. Just stick to the program they give you—that's all they expect us to do anyway. It really won't matter." I can remember feeling angry and shocked when I first heard this statement. I couldn't believe that a teacher would tell a novice, pre-service teacher not to believe in her students—to see teaching as following a script as opposed to students learning. I was upset to hear a teacher have such a negative attitude towards children who sat in her class ready to learn. I immediately wrote it down in my notebook, completely in awe that a teacher could believe this. Here was my student, preparing to become a teacher, and the first message she hears from her master teacher is to give up on a group of students for no other reason than the fact that they were English language learners.

I often came back to this quote and reflected on my work as a teacher and now as a teacher educator. I understood the master teacher's frustration, but could not get past the idea that these were children who deserved a great education, as every child does. I remember thinking that I could have been the student in this class. I was a bilingual student. I looked like the students in this master teacher's class. I remember thinking that I wished my own children would never be in this teacher's class. These were not my own children, but it was someone else's child who was entrusted in the hands of a teacher.

This experience, as well as many others, made me realize how important it is to reach out to teachers and send the message that all students, including English language learners, deserve a quality and meaningful education. All students are capable of learning, and all teachers must remember their role in not only educating a child, but preparing the next generation of model citizens, leaders, and members of a democratic, diverse society. What messages are we sending to our students when we expect them to fail before we even start teaching? Teaching is not an easy job, but it is an important job that we are fortunate to acquire.

I understand that as teachers we become overwhelmed with state, district, and school mandates. We can often feel powerless and ineffective. I can remember thinking that I was not doing enough as a teacher to ensure that all of my students received a high-quality education as I had received. I really enjoyed school and felt that I had received a great education. Yet, as a teacher, literacy coach, professor, and professional developer, I have seen students sitting silently, disengaged from their learning. I have seen thousands of students fall through the cracks and reach minimal levels of academic achievement. Data has shown that large numbers of English language learners drop out of school every year. "Transcript data from L.A. city schools allowed an analysis of graduation rates in 2004 for those English language learners who were enrolled in the ninth grade in 2000...only 27% remained in school and graduated with their class in the district in 2004" (Gandara and Contreras 2009, 45). I have seen students get stuck at an intermediate level of English language acquisition, unable to develop high levels of academic English for academic success. These are some of the disheartening realities of what we see in the education of English language learners.

I share these facts to remind teachers that there is a need to focus our attention on the education of English language learners. Through this book and my work as a teacher educator, I am committed to supporting teachers and maintaining my position that English language learners are brilliant and ready to be challenged in their thinking and learning. We must maintain high expectations and a high-quality curriculum for English language learners. I understand that English language learners have unique needs that can create greater challenges for teachers. I also believe that we became teachers because we believe in children and in ourselves as teachers. We have to turn our attention toward ourselves as educators. We need to revisit our thinking and learning pertaining to language development and explore pedagogical approaches for diverse student populations. We need to begin to make better instructional decisions as teachers of English language learners. Our classrooms must be filled with talk and interaction around challenging content. If we expect English language learners to develop academic language and to make meaning from challenging curricula, we must work hard to learn all that we can about how to teach them effectively.

This book will take you through specific strategies, methods, instructional approaches, resources, activities, and reflective questions to support your work with English language learners. The chapters in this book are the following:

- Chapter 1, *Guiding Principles*, shares what I have learned from working with English language learners year to year.

- Chapter 2, *Language Development*, highlights the process of learning a second language and how teachers can facilitate language development.

- Chapter 3, *Academic Language*, reminds us of the complexities of the language that students must develop in all content areas to be successful in school.

- Chapter 4, *Creating a Language-Rich Environment,* continues with a look at learning environments and how we can set the appropriate context for learning a new language and learning through a second language.

- Chapter 5, *Literacy Instruction for English Language Learners: Essential Elements*, explores literacy development and what it means to provide a quality language arts program for English language learners. Then, it delves into the role of language throughout our instructional day.

- Chapter 6, *Developing Language Across the Curriculum*, provides readers with a clear understanding of English Language Development (ELD) and content ELD and its relationship to Academic Language Development (ALD). Understanding the purpose of ELD and how it fits within content area instruction helps teachers support English language learners throughout the day.

This book is really a reflection on what I have learned from working with English language learners and from English language learners themselves. I have taught dual-language, waiver-to-basic, English-only, Spanish as a second language, Structured English Immersion (SEI), and Gifted and Talented Education (GATE) ranging from kindergarten to eighth grade, and have continued my work as a consultant for high school teachers of English language learners. I taught using scripted standards-based programs, no programs, the Four-Blocks® Literacy Model, high-stakes testing and accountability, and various other state and district mandates. We have all had similar experiences and we have all learned from each and every one of them. At times I was stressed, confused, and exhausted from one instructional context to the next. I struggled and succeeded inside the political arena where I was teaching. But when I took time to reflect on my teaching, I realized what a blessing it was to learn something new every year and extend my understanding of teaching and learning. We often hear the saying "We never stop learning," and as teachers this is an understatement. I strongly believe that every year we learn more about ourselves as teachers. Our students help us become better teachers and teach us the life lessons of being great educators.

CHAPTER 1

Guiding Principles

"Our language is a reflection of ourselves. A language is an exact reflection of the character and growth of its speakers."

— César Chávez

My Journey as a Bilingual Child

My journey as a teacher of language has been dynamic, challenging, and humbling at times. Growing up bilingual, I never thought about the complexities of language. When at home, I would speak Spanish to my parents, listen to Spanish-speaking radio stations, and watch *novelas* and game shows in Spanish. When visiting family, additional models of Spanish surrounded me. We were always a close family, and someone was always correcting your Spanish during conversation. I felt like I was always learning new words or the appropriate words for a given context. As a child, I would just correct my Spanish as directed, not really thinking about the mistakes I had made. I was acquiring and learning language in an authentic setting. I was surrounded by cues from my environment, making language comprehensible.

I never attended school in Spanish—just learned it from family, television, and print. It was not until high school that I finally started learning about the Spanish language—in my Spanish foreign-language class. I can remember a very traditional grammar-translation approach, where we would read a dialogue, answer questions, memorize vocabulary lists, translate sentences, conjugate verbs, and learn grammar rules. We never actually *spoke* in Spanish; we learned *about* the Spanish language. What I think I learned most from my Spanish classes was how to write properly in Spanish. I could already read in Spanish and wrote fairly well because learning to read and write in English transferred to learning to read and write in Spanish. What I had to learn were particular grammar rules, like the haunting accent marks that I never could figure out and how to punctuate dialogue. The concepts were the same as those in English, but I had to learn how to mark my text properly. All the language I had brought from my home experiences with Spanish made learning about the language fairly easy. And all I had learned in school about reading and writing in English had transferred to my learning of academic Spanish.

My Experiences as a Teacher of English Language Learners

Throughout my journey as a teacher, I enjoyed watching and learning from students in a variety of settings. They taught me that they can reach high levels of academic success and language development across settings with the right support and instructional decision making. These early experiences with language helped prepare me for my first full-time teaching experience as a dual-language first-grade teacher. It was an amazing experience. I had a 50/50 model where half of my class was English dominant and the other half was Spanish dominant. In this model, students serve as language learners for one another. Language arts and mathematics were taught in English, and the remaining core subjects were taught in Spanish. Every day, students would receive half of their instruction in Spanish and the other half in English. As a classroom community, we pledged not to code switch during these times and supported one another in our language struggles and successes. For example, if it was Spanish time and a student needed to use the restroom, he or she would ask in Spanish. Then English time came around, and if the student needed to go again, he or she would ask in English. The same was true for everything we read and wrote. All forms of communication were in the language at hand. We were committed to becoming a bilingual classroom community.

This was the year that I saw how powerful bilingual education can be for students. By December, all of my students were reading and writing in both languages. They wrote amazing stories that went on for pages and began reading chapter books by January. I was in awe! The transfer of their cognitive skills from English to Spanish was so natural and they were so comfortable with one another that they felt safe making errors and being models for one another. I too became more confident in my work as a teacher of language. Through my own experiences and those of my students, I felt strongly about the concept of transfer. I also learned the following about being a teacher of language and language learners:

- Cognitive skills and concepts learned in a primary language transfer to learning a second language.

- Content and skills must be taught through meaningful, authentic experiences.

- English language learners must feel connected to their language. In other words, learning must be meaningful and relevant to students' lives.

- English language learners need to feel safe trying out language and serving as language models for one another.

- English language learners are brilliant as they navigate two languages to reach high levels of academic success.

- English language learners need to feel that they are members of a learning community, where everyone is a novice, an apprentice, and an expert.

- Quality bilingual programs best support English language learners to develop high levels of academic achievement in both languages.

- Rigorous, quality teaching is appropriate for all English language learners.

- Challenging curriculum is appropriate for all English language learners.

- All English language learners are capable of reaching high levels of academic achievement.

- Teachers must believe that all English language learners are capable of high levels of academic English and school success.

This list represents what I believe to be true about how to support English language learners in diverse instructional contexts. It is a foundation I use as I continue to learn from students and now from teachers who have taken on the rewarding challenge of working alongside English language learners. It is important to learn about the primary languages students bring to the classroom and to build upon their early foundations with language. The more connections you can make between one language to another, the easier it is to transfer the skills and knowledge.

I went on to teach middle school and taught sixth- through eighth-grade humanities (English and social studies) and Spanish as a foreign language. When teaching Spanish, I began teaching from a traditional grammar-translation approach. This was my experience in my own Spanish foreign-language class. I had my students reading dialogues, answering comprehension questions, studying vocabulary lists, conjugating verbs, translating sentences, and learning grammar rules. But as I reflected on my teaching, I realized my students were not learning Spanish. They were not making meaning from their learning. They spoke in English and were just learning about Spanish. They were not learning to become speakers of Spanish. My students did not have opportunities to apply their learning or to speak in Spanish.

At first I was confused. A grammar-translation approach seemed easy and worked for me. I was able to make meaning when I read passages, and I used what I learned in vocabulary and grammar to improve my own Spanish when speaking to family. It was meaningful for me because I already spoke Spanish, so I used my learning as a way to improve my own language skills. This was not the case for my students. Only a handful of them were bilingual.

I decided to radically change my teaching practices and search for new ways of teaching Spanish as a foreign language. I wanted my students to become speakers of the language, not simply become knowledgeable in the language. I decided to engage students in cultural studies about Spanish speaking countries, converse with them only in Spanish, play games instead of taking vocabulary tests, and read and write in Spanish together. The students came into the room and we moved desks around to see eye-to-eye and engage in authentic conversations—*in Spanish*—about course texts. We talked about their own culture. We studied Latin American history. I felt empowered as a teacher of language! I had found a way to truly develop language and make learning meaningful and relevant to my students.

Classroom Connection

I vividly remember one day in Spanish class when a student voiced what my curricular decisions meant to him. Tomás was an eighth grader of Puerto Rican descent. He was English dominant and shared that he could understand Spanish but was not confident enough to speak it. During class one day, he stopped me in the middle of a lesson. We had been talking about the history of Puerto Rico and its relationship with the United States. At first I was a little taken aback, wondering why he had asked me to stop. The class became silent and all eyes and ears were on Tomás. He quickly apologized and shared that he did not mean to be disrespectful or disruptive, but he had something he really wanted to share. Tomás said, "Hey, Ms. Mora, why hasn't anyone ever taught us this before? This is who I am. I don't get it—why am I like 13 before I ever hear about this? Thank you." I knew I had made a difference. This was the student in the school whom everyone had dismissed and called the troublemaker. He had been suspended multiple times and was often truant. But he never missed a homework assignment, passed all of his exams, and created stellar projects in my class. His report card read all Fs but one A in Spanish. Though it may not have mattered to others that he passed Spanish over other core content areas, it mattered that he had made a connection. I realized how important it was for students to be able to connect to their learning.

Tomás made me a better teacher because he reminded me that teaching is about getting to know your students and building upon the foundations set by their families and community. Teaching is about discovering new ways of connecting your content in a way that is engaging and meaningful to students. Too often we hear about the large numbers of students dropping out of school as early as sixth grade. One of the primary reasons is that students disengage from school. They do not see the relevance of what they are learning to their lives or their future. They need a reason to be there; they are looking for a purpose for coming to school every day. If we can help them feel successful, find ways of making real-world connections, and engage them in authentic learning opportunities, we stand a better chance of encouraging them to stay in school.

My journey as a teacher of language took another turn, and again I found myself back in first grade teaching a waiver-to-basic Spanish-English class. A waiver-to-basic class was a regular first-grade class that was taught in English but included students whose parents had signed a waiver requesting bilingual education for their child. The challenge became teaching 15 of my 20 students in English and the remaining five, who had waivers, in Spanish. This was the year I learned about the power of flexible grouping, small-group rotations, and how important workshop models are for differentiating instruction. This was a very tricky year that took a lot of dynamic planning.

Having the two different programs in my class, English-only and bilingual waiver-to-basic, I was able to see the impact of the programs. I saw how the language of instruction affected students participating in English-only versus bilingual programs. This came about in 1998 when California voters passed Proposition 227, English for the Children. As a result, many bilingual programs were eliminated and English language learners were instructed entirely in English through Structured English Immersion (SEI). This was the case at my school, with the exception of a few classes that had waiver students. And though I had five waiver students, the remaining students were also English language learners.

Based on Proposition 227 and opponents of bilingual education, the expectation was that my English language learners in the SEI program would outperform the waiver-to-basic group. However, the reverse was true. My waiver-to-basic students dramatically outperformed my English-only group. All five students in the waiver-to-basic program, receiving Spanish language arts and math scored the highest on our standardized measures in both English and Spanish. This was a group that had started off the year below grade level and below my English learners in the SEI program. Research on bilingual education repeatedly supports this finding (Willig 1985; Greene 1998; Gandara and Contreras 2009). Students in quality bilingual programs do better academically in the long run in both English and Spanish. I had experienced firsthand the effectiveness of bilingual education.

What I learned that year was that a *quality* bilingual program was the best program model for English language learners. I also saw a connection between this program and my own experience—learning language in a primary language and then transferring to learning a second language. The same was true for these students. In a careful analysis of two major research studies focusing on the education of English learners, Claude Goldenberg (2008) shared, "With respect to English language learners, a substantial body of research by both CREDE [Center for Research on Education, Diversity, and Excellence] and NLP [National Literacy Panel] research suggests that literacy and other skills and knowledge transfer across languages (15)." However, what I had yet to learn was how to support English language learners in SEI and English-only settings when bilingual education was not an option.

Yet again, I found myself challenged as a teacher of language and spent a decade working with English language learners in SEI and English-only settings. I learned so many wonderful, challenging instructional strategies and methods in my credential program and had practiced them in my previous years as a bilingual educator. I attended the latest conferences and picked up a plethora of strategies and ideas for developing critical and creative thinkers and writers. But when confronted with this new instructional setting, I learned how important it was to tailor instruction to meet the unique language needs of students.

Reinventing Myself as a Teacher for English-Only Settings

After years of working with English language learners I began to wonder, "What was missing? What had I understood about diversity? What had I understood about how students learn? Did I think about how students who speak a language other than English learn? Did I think about diversity as a resource for teaching and learning? How can I support my students in a way that leads to high levels of academic success?" I began to read all that I could about working with English language learners, and too often I found instructional practices to be predominantly skills-based and reductionist. I became discouraged. I kept thinking what a disservice we were providing to these students. I had seen how intelligent English language learners were—how complex, different, and capable they all were. I learned how brilliant English language learners are as they navigate through two languages. It is not easy to learn a language and have to learn through a new language at the same time. It takes high levels of thinking and intelligence to conquer this task. I knew that a bilingual child was capable of so much more than what my reading indicated.

I decided to continue my education by studying English language learners in English-only settings, reinventing myself as a teacher. I revisited effective programs and high-quality methods for teaching English language learners in bilingual settings. I focused on instructional practices that supported English language learners when English was the language of instruction. I recalled what I had learned through my own experiences working with English language learners in diverse settings. I studied high-quality methods and approaches for English-dominant students and thought about how I might tailor these types of programs to meet the needs of English language learners in English-only settings.

English language learners deserve a challenging curriculum that exposes them to quality literature, authentic writing experiences, inquiry-based content instruction, and high levels of thinking and production. Through this book, I share with you what I have learned through these experiences, highlighting instructional practices that I have researched, implemented, and reflected upon and that lead to high levels of academic success for English language learners in SEI and English-only settings.

Since my work as a full-time classroom teacher, I have spent years training novice and experienced teachers of English language learners through various capacities. I have been both saddened and overjoyed when I hear stories about teachers of English language learners. Stories range from feelings of helplessness to feelings of confidence as teachers find the most effective ways to support their students. I have also been struck by the negative comments and attitudes that I have heard about English language learners—comments that undermine their abilities and their beliefs—which presume that they cannot accomplish certain tasks or can only achieve minimal standards. As a bilingual child and now a bilingual teacher, these types of statements break my heart. My goal for this book is to help educators see that when given the right support, English language learners are capable of reaching high levels of academic achievement and deserve to be educated in a culture of high expectations. This book is a record of what I have learned working with English language learners and teachers of English language learners within a culture of high expectations and high outcomes in academic English and overall academic success. I share this book with you in the hopes that you too will feel empowered by the opportunities to learn from and support English language learners.

Reflection Questions

1. What are your experiences as a teacher of language? What have you learned from those experiences?

2. What do you know to be true about teaching English language learners?

3. What challenges have you had as a teacher of English language learners? What have you learned from those challenges?

4. What resources are available to you as a teacher of language and of English language learners? How have you used those resources?

Language Development

"The limits of my language are the limits of my world."

— *Ludwig Wittgenstein*

Language is powerful because it allows people to access knowledge. It is how we communicate and learn from others. It is how we make meaning from text and share our thoughts with the world through written and oral forms. Language is powerful because it connects us to one another. It connects us to our families, our community, and our friends. According to Merriam-Webster, language has been defined as "a body of words and the systems for their use common to a people who are of the same community or nation, the same geographical area, or the same cultural tradition." As simple as this may seem, language is complex—and for those of us who have tried to learn a second language or teach language, we have experienced the complexities of language.

Language Acquisition

Children have an amazing ability to acquire a first language quickly and subconsciously. Krashen and Terrell (1983) discuss the difference between acquiring language and learning language.

They share that "language acquisition is a 'natural' way to develop linguistic ability, and is a subconscious process…(26)." This natural process is how children initially develop language. Through exposure to contextualized language, as children communicate with the world around them, they naturally acquire language. They are not aware that they are acquiring language. They are more concerned with communicating with their surroundings. This process is pretty amazing when we think about the sophistication of a child's language before he or she even enters school. Children may develop a rich vocabulary, a strong use of syntax, and a distinct phonological system of language. They begin school ready to deepen their language development by learning about language and continuing the acquisition process. The challenge, however, comes when the language of instruction is not the primary language of the learner.

English language learners have developed a complex level of language development in a primary language other than English. They too have spent their early years exposed to rich language models, practiced using language across contexts, and developed a strong language identity. Just as with all students, school serves as a vehicle for deepening their language and continuing the acquisition process. What is different—aside from students obviously needing to learn a new language—is how teachers can support English language learners.

Teachers need to listen to their students. They need to take note of the language that students bring to the classroom. This includes the phonology, orthography, syntax, vocabulary, and discourse that students learned and developed in their primary language along with what they know and can do in English.

Language Transfer

Jim Cummins (1984) has found that the development of a primary language can help in learning a new language. My personal experience as a language learner, as well as my work with English language learners supported my understanding of this transfer.

Classroom Connection

In my first year of teaching an SEI class, I had a new student, Ricardo, who had only been in the United States for a week. Previously, he had attended school in Mexico and had already learned to read and write in Spanish. During a small guided-reading session, I pulled a group of students to read *In a Dark, Dark, House* by Jennifer Dussling. Ricardo picked up the book we were reading and started flipping through the pages, looking at the pictures, and simply browsing the text. Once we all settled in, I noticed he began reading the book by sounding out the words using his knowledge of Spanish orthography (the spelling system) and phonology (the sound system). He sounded out the entire text, stopping often to look at the pictures before reading on. He was using decoding skills and picture cues to read. Ricardo had not read in English before, but he did not have to relearn the concept of sound-symbol relationships for sounding out words. He had already learned to read in Spanish. He transferred his knowledge of reading in Spanish to reading in English.

Classroom Connection

On another occasion, I observed a fifth-grade class during a unit on "Heritage." The teacher posted pictures of family celebrations around the classroom, many of which the students could relate to. She asked the students to walk around the room with partners, discussing what they saw in the pictures. Students shared, "This is a picture of what looks like a birthday party. There is a cake, presents, lots of people, and kids are smiling and look like they are having fun." "It's Fourth of July. Lots of fireworks and sparkles. I see a flag, too." The gallery walk went on for about five minutes and then students returned to their seats. The teacher asked some students to share what they had learned with their partners. Following the brief class discussion, the teacher presented the words *tradition*, *celebration*, and *customs*. The teacher asked the class to share their understanding of the three words. One student said, "*tradiciones*, like when we go to my grandma's house every Sunday for breakfast." Another student shared, "We always have tamales on Christmas, too; that's a tradition." The discussion went on with students sharing examples that demonstrated an understanding of the meaning of the words. Without explicitly teaching the words, the students had relied upon conceptual knowledge developed in a primary language that transferred to their learning vocabulary in English. They were already familiar with the concepts; they just needed to learn the labels (words) in English.

In the fifth-grade example, students also demonstrated an understanding of *cognates*, words that are similar in spelling, meaning, and pronunciation from one language to another. The words *traditions*, *celebrations*, and *customs* are all cognates with the Spanish words *tradiciones*, *celebraciones*, and *costumbres*. Cummins (1984) referred to this transfer as the *Common Underlying Proficiency (CUP) hypothesis*. The CUP hypothesis stipulates that both languages are working through the same processing system. The deeper conceptual understanding and skills we learn in one language does not change when learning a second language. The surface-level output is what changes. Meaning, what we say or write (output) changes as we share our thinking and use our skills to make sense of the new language. This requires a well-developed primary-language, both conversational and academic. When students have strong primary language literacy skills, they can use them to learn to read in a second language. This is true for all languages. English language learners can call upon content knowledge, skills, conceptual knowledge, and strategies learned through a primary language when developing a second language (Goldenberg 2008). As teachers, we need to understand CUP as a critical piece for supporting English language learners. We need to think about how we can use the knowledge and language that students develop in their first language to support their learning *of* and *in* English.

Learning a Language

Learning a new language and trying to learn in a second language is very difficult. Imagine sitting in a chemistry class where the language of instruction is French, and you only speak English. You are trying to learn chemistry and French at the same time. Then the teacher tells you that there will be a written exam at the end of the week, and you are still trying to figure out what was said in the first five minutes of class. This is what our English language learners encounter every day in English-only settings. They are submerged in English, trying to keep up academically and develop language. A challenge, yes; an impossible task, no. The more we can learn about the language-learning process, the better we can support English language learners to reach high levels of academic achievement in English. This includes reflecting on our own language-learning experiences, exploring the literature on language learning, and utilizing our resources to create effective learning environments.

In my experience working with pre-service teachers, I often begin our study on educating English language learners by thinking about our own processes and experiences as language learners. I ask them to reflect on the following questions: *How did you learn language? What helped you learn language? What challenges have you had learning language? What language-learning strategies have you used in your own language journey?* We begin with a personal reflection, and then share with our partners and search for similarities and differences. As a class, we make a list of what we have learned from our own experiences as language learners. The following table, *Language-Learning Experiences,* shares some ideas my pre-service teachers have taught me about their own language learning.

Language-Learning Experiences

Received support from:	<ul><li>family members</li><li>language models</li><li>television</li><li>rich contexts (language was visible)</li><li>friends</li><li>books</li><li>resources (e.g., dictionaries, Internet)</li><li>strong sense of community—feeling safe to make errors</li></ul>

Language-Learning Experiences *(cont.)*

Challenges I faced:	<ul><li>holding conversations with native speakers</li><li>comprehending abstract concepts</li><li>limited text support (e.g., pictures, charts, graphs)</li><li>phonology (primary and secondary languages have different sound-symbol systems)</li><li>lacking opportunities to practice using the new language</li><li>not seeing language in action</li></ul>
Language-learning strategies I used:	<ul><li>gaining knowledge of syntax from primary language</li><li>gaining knowledge of stories</li><li>gaining knowledge of phonology (sounds and symbols) from primary language</li><li>using context clues to make meaning</li><li>gaining knowledge of content, ideas, and concepts</li></ul>

We use this information to think about how we can support English language learners in the classroom. It is a beginning in the process of becoming a teacher of language. We want to build upon these experiences to make sense of the language development.

Learning a Second Language

As an educator, I have read a plethora of research and literature that agrees and disagrees on how to support students learning a second language. Taking what I have read and connecting it to my work in classrooms with English language learners, I have come to rely on the work of many notable researchers. These scholars have for years been working in the field of second-language acquisition and teaching English language learners. In the table on pages 34–36, I have noted key researchers and resources I refer to in my work toward understanding second-language acquisition.

Literature on Learning Language and Teaching English Language Learners

Researcher	What I Have Learned	Resource
Robin Scarcella	• Students need large quantities of exposure to language. • Students need many opportunities to practice using the target language. • Students need explicit instruction on how to use the target language. • Students need feedback on their language usage.	*Accelerating Academic English: A Focus on the English Learner* (2003)
Richard Anderson and William Nagy	• Students learn approximately 2,000–3,500 words a year; therefore, we need to provide opportunities for incidental and explicit vocabulary instruction. • Teaching morphology empowers students to make meaning of new words.	The Vocabulary Conundrum (1992)
Isabel Beck, Margaret McKeown, and Linda Kucan	• Word knowledge is complex. • Teaching should focus on high-utility words that appear frequently in a wide variety of texts and across contexts. • Students need direct instruction of purposefully selected vocabulary words • Students need playful and varied opportunities to use words.	*Bringing Words to Life: Robust Vocabulary Instruction* (2002) *Creating Robust Vocabulary: Frequently Asked Questions and Extended Examples* (2008)

Literature on Learning Language and Teaching English Language Learners *(cont.)*

Researcher	What I Have Learned	Resource
Louisa Cook Moats	• Language involves phonology, orthography, morphology, syntax, semantics, pragmatics, and discourse structure. • Students need to understand all levels of language and how they are interrelated to make meaning from written and spoken language. • Teachers need to understand language to support students' literacy development.	*Speech to Print: Language Essentials for Teachers* (2000)
David and Yvonne Freeman	• Our teaching of language is greatly influenced by our beliefs about how children learn language and its application to second-language acquisition. • Understanding the components of a language helps teachers facilitate language learning.	*Essential Linguistics: What You Need to Know to Teach Reading, ESL, Spelling, Phonics, and Grammar* (2004)
Pauline Gibbons	• Teachers must have clear language objectives to support academic language development. • Motivation is critical in learning to learn in a second language. • Questions teachers ask are important in creating situations where certain language patterns may occur. • Students need explicit language instruction as well as academic language development across the curriculum.	*Learning to Learn in a Second Language* (1993) *English Learners, Academic Literacy, and Thinking: Learning in the Challenge Zone* (2009)

Literature on Learning Language and Teaching English Language Learners *(cont.)*

Researcher	What I Have Learned	Resource
Lilia Sarmiento, Eugenia Mora-Flores, and Dolores Beltran	• Effective language instruction provides students with opportunities to use vocabulary and functions and forms of language in diverse contexts to build fluency. • Students need to be involved in learning experiences that provide opportunities for thought, talk, and interaction.	Thinking and Doing Approach to Language Development: Science and ELD (2010)
Stephen Krashen and Tracy Terrell	• Students need to feel safe learning language. • High-anxiety settings hinder language acquisition. • Language must be understood to be acquired.	*The Natural Approach: Language Acquisition in the Classroom* (1983)
Jim Cummins	• The complex language systems we developed in a primary language support learning a second language. • Conceptual knowledge transfers from one language to another. • Becoming fluent in a language involves both conversational proficiency as well as academic language proficiency in a second language.	The Construct of Language Proficiency in Bilingual Education (1980) Wanted: A Theoretical Framework for Relating Language Proficiency to Academic Achievement Among Bilingual Students (1984)

The research on second-language acquisition has guided my work as a teacher of English language learners. It has helped me understand what it means to develop a second language, the complexities of language, and how to support students learning a second language. In addition, I have learned that to support English language learners, we must also understand how language builds towards proficiency.

Language Development Levels

How language development is monitored and identified varies across the country. In my work with districts, I have heard terms such as second-language acquisition levels (SLA) and English language development levels (ELD). In both cases, there are five distinct levels identified, beginning with an initial exposure to the language—often called the "pre-production" or "silent stage" (level 1)—and ending with a "native-like fluency stage" (level 5). In my experience, most researchers in the area of second language use the term second-language acquisition, as noted in the table on pages 38–40, *Second-Language Acquisition Levels*. In practice, districts may use a variety of terms or labels when referring to levels of language development. What is important is that teachers understand what students bring to the learning experience in terms of language and build toward the next stage in the language-development process. In addition, it is important to keep in mind how we scaffold instruction for English language learners and the questions we should be asking that lead to expected student responses.

Second-Language Acquisition Levels

Second-Language (L2) Acquisition Level	Expected Student Engagement	Teacher Support

Pre-production (first 3–6 months)	– Listen attentively.
	– Focus on comprehension.
	– Have an emerging receptive vocabulary.
	– May not verbalize.
	– May repeat what they hear (parroting).
	– Can respond using:
	  • one-word responses
	  • drawing
	  • writing in a primary language (when applicable)
	  • creating graphic designs
	  • copying
	  • pointing
	  • circling responses
	  • underlining their answer
	  • matching items, pictures, ideas
		– Speak clearly and intentionally with intonation, gestures, and phrasing.
		– Use precise survival language. (Open the book.)
		– Recast appropriate language.
		– Provide visuals.
		– Use Total Physical Response.
		– Prompt students with:
		  • Show me…
		  • Circle the…
		  • Where is...?
		  • Who has…?
		  • Point to…
		– Read aloud to students.
		– Use music to practice phonology and learn new words.

Early Production (6 months–1 year)	– Continue to develop a receptive vocabulary and use an active, expressive vocabulary.
	– Continue to focus on comprehension.
	– Use simple sentences and stock expressions to express needs, wants, and thoughts.
	– Participate using key words or phrases.
	– Use present-tense verbs.
	– Demonstrate their learning by:
	  • naming
	  • labeling
	  • answering *who, what, when, where* questions
	  • drawing
	  • copying
	  • grouping and labeling
	  • selecting
	  • matching
	  • acting out responses (miming)
	  • pointing
		– Speak using compound, complex sentences with the support of gestures, expressions, and visuals.
		– Ask yes/no and either/or questions.
		– Present information through:
		  • lists
		  • labels
		  • pictures and realia
		  • graphic organizers
		  • charts
		  • graphs
		  • read-alouds
		– Use predictable texts.
		– Use text with rich contextual clues.
		– Scaffold writing using prompts and sentence starters when appropriate.
		– Recast, do not correct.

Second-Language Acquisition Levels *(cont.)*

Second-Language (L2) Acquisition Level	Expected Student Engagement	Teacher Support

Speech Emergent (1–3 years)	– Increase comprehension.
	– Initiate short conversations.
	– Use simple sentences.
	– Expand vocabulary.
	– Continue grammatical errors.
	– Present thinking and learning by:
	  • recalling
	  • retelling/telling
	  • describing
	  • explaining
	  • comparing
	  • sequencing
	  • using dialogue
	  • demonstrating
	  • role-playing
	– Write and develop fluency (journals).
		– Facilitate cooperative-group tasks.
		– Prompt student thinking with questions that ask:
		  • Why?
		  • How?
		  • Explain.
		– Do choral reading.
		– Model the use of graphic organizers to share thinking and learning.
		– Scaffold written discourse for students.
		– Utilize journals.

Intermediate Fluency (3–7 years)	– Demonstrate conversational proficiency.
	– Express opinions.
	– Share their thinking orally and in writing.
	– Ask clarifying questions.
	– Synthesize information heard and read.
	– Improve comprehension.
	– Have fewer grammatical errors.
	– Predict
	– Narrate
	– Describe
	– Explain
	– Summarize
	– Express opinions.
	– Debate/defend their thinking.
	– Write creatively.
	– Write across genres (focusing on written discourse).
	– Role-play
		– Model sophisticated language and academic language.
		– Probe thinking with questions that ask:
		  • Should…?
		  • Could…?
		  • Would…?
		  • What if…?
		  • Can…?
		  • Why…?
		  • If…then…?
		– Provide opportunities for peer discussions.
		– Facilitate cooperative-group work.
		– Model writing across the curriculum; focus on written discourse across genres.
		– Provide exposure to varied sources of text.

Second-Language Acquisition Levels *(cont.)*

Second-Language (L2) Acquisition Level	Expected Student Engagement	Teacher Support
Advanced Fluency/Native-like Fluency (5–10 years)	– Have near native-like fluency. – Demonstrate critical and creative thinking. – Express abstract thinking orally and in writing. – Read a wide variety of texts across the content areas. – Write a variety of text types and genres.	– Provoke deep levels of thinking with prompts such as: • decide if • infer • evaluate • critique • determine the importance

Adapted from Hearne (2000), Collier (1987), and Krashen and Terrell (1983)

Conclusion

Our work as teachers of language begins by understanding language development. We want to examine what we know about how people learn language and what it means to become fluent in a language. We can begin by thinking about our own experiences and what helped us learn language. This helps us to understand the language-learning process. Coupled with our own language experiences are those of our students. Understanding what English language learners bring to their second-language learning experience helps us build upon their foundational knowledge and skills to reach higher levels of second-language acquisition. We need to understand the literature on second-language acquisition and what is involved in learning in and about a language. This knowledge of language and language instruction helps us to understand how to support English language learners.

Reflection Questions

1. What were your experiences as a learner of language, and how do these experiences impact your work as a teacher of language?

2. What challenges have you faced learning a new language? What helped you overcome those challenges?

3. What have you learned about second-language acquisition?

4. What does it mean to be fluent in a language?

Academic Language

"Language shapes the way we think, and determines what we can think about."

— Benjamin Lee Whorf

We have talked a great deal about language development and supporting students in their acquisition of language itself. However, what makes the language-learning experience a challenge for English language learners is that they will have to develop content knowledge in English while learning the English language. Too often, we find English language learners getting stuck at an intermediate, conversational level of second-language acquisition. They sound fluent in everyday casual conversations, yet they continue to struggle in school. What they often lack is the *academic language* necessary for school success.

Jim Cummins (1980) discussed the difference between students' conversational proficiency and academic language proficiency. Basic Interpersonal Communication Skills (BICS) is the language we need to engage in social conversations. For English language learners, this is often the level of proficiency reached at a speech-emergent level of second-language acquisition. Students sound fluent as they interact with friends. They can understand directions, verbally express their thinking at basic levels of comprehension, and write for a variety of purposes. Building upon BICS, Cummins further discusses the notion of Cognitive Academic Language Proficiency (CALP). This is the level of language development where students are able to understand concrete and abstract language and express their thinking across the curriculum. It is the language students need to comprehend and use for academic success.

We often think about academic language solely as the content-specific vocabulary of a discipline. Though it does include vocabulary, it also includes the functions and forms that cross disciplines and are more common in one field versus another. It includes high-frequency vocabulary that is used across the curriculum by students to share their thinking and learning. It further includes building the fluency in the language to be able to effectively communicate your thinking to others both orally and in writing. **Academic language includes vocabulary, the functions and forms of language, and the fluency one needs to demonstrate thinking and learning across the curriculum.**

Vocabulary

Vocabulary involves developing high-frequency vocabulary that students can use across the domains to develop an expressive and receptive vocabulary (Beck and McKeown 1991; Anderson and Nagy 1992; Lesaux and Kieffer 2010). Students need to build their understanding of words and their use of these new words for retention. The goal is to help students not only understand words, but also make them part of their own personal lexicon. We want students to use words appropriately when speaking and writing for a variety of purposes and across contexts.

Traditional vocabulary instruction focuses on receptive vocabulary, providing students opportunities to look up words, explore word meanings, and compare meanings across words—such as with synonyms and antonyms. What they do not get enough time to do is practice using new words when they write or engage in conversations with others. Most of us have a higher receptive vocabulary than expressive vocabulary. We find ourselves at a loss for words at times because we do not have the vocabulary to express what it is we want to share. This is a greater challenge if students do not have opportunities outside of school to practice their English. It limits their exposure to words and usage, which in turn hinders their expressive vocabulary development. We must provide students with ample opportunities to engage in thoughtful dialogue and discussions with peers throughout the day. This is a critical part of English language development, providing English language learners with varied opportunities to use their acquired vocabulary.

Students need opportunities to use high utility words. These would be words that are used often in academic settings and can transfer across the curriculum. For example, a vocabulary word such as *transformation* can be practiced and used in different content areas. Students can talk about the transformation of a character, a science experiment, an event in history and beyond school. Beck and McKeown (1991) refer to these types of words as Tier 2 words; words that have high instructional potential and high utility. In addition to high utility words, students also need to understand and use content specific words to guide their learning across the curriculum. These words, however, may not have the same frequency of use as high utility words because students may only be exposed to them during a unit of study.

I frequently ask my students to think about their own personal language-learning experiences. Most of us can relate to our experiences learning a second language in high school. We spent hours translating dialogues, memorizing vocabulary lists, and engaging in grammar-based lessons. We would do well in class, thinking we had learned a great deal, yet to our surprise, we were tongue-tied and found that we struggled to engage in a conversation with someone because though we had learned the rules and understood what we read and heard. This is what happens to our own students. Without the application of their word learning, they struggle to develop their vocabulary.

Functions and Forms of Language

Language functions can be defined as the purpose for using language. Why are we using language? Is it to compare, describe, or persuade? Students need opportunities to use language for a variety of purposes. ELD instruction involves explicit teacher modeling of selected language functions and opportunities for students to practice functions of language. Functions of language are directly connected to language forms. The forms of language, also referred to as frames of language, are the structures of language used to fulfill a function. For example, if we ask students to describe a mammal, they might use frames such as:

"The _____ is_____." "It has_____."
"It looks _____."

Examples of functions and forms of language can be found in the Appendix on pages 152–157.

During ELD, students are given opportunities to hear functions and forms of language and practice using them to develop fluency. What is important to remember is that students will need opportunities to develop and use forms of language appropriate for their individual language levels. Thinking back to the example of describing a mammal, students at level 3 should no longer be modeled or allowed to simply use forms such as:

"The _____ is _____." "It has_____."

We need to challenge them and help them to reach the next level of language development by providing new forms of language such as:

"Salient characteristics of a _____ include _____ and _____." "The _____ demonstrates _____."
"A/An _____ has particular attributes, such as _____."

We often find that many English language learners get stuck at the intermediate level of English language development. I have found that part of the reason lies in the lack of understanding what we can expect of students at the different levels of ELD. We need to listen carefully to our students. We must take note of the language that they are bringing to the learning experience and take them further. Teachers can do a wonderful job providing opportunities for explicit language instruction, but if they are giving students language opportunities they already possess, they are simply practicing and not developing higher levels of language.

This is a general explanation based on my experience as a teacher of English as a Second Language (ESL) and ELD and in my work as a professional developer in ELD. There are a great deal of variations in the definition and understanding of both ELD and ESL. What is important is that we understand the need to provide students with explicit language instruction where the objectives focus on the English language itself and students are provided opportunities to practice using English for a variety of purposes. Ultimately, as students are provided multiple opportunities to hear, speak, read, and write vocabulary, and practice functions and forms of language, they will develop oral and written fluency.

Academic Language Development

Academic language development happens every day, as students are constantly encountering language challenges. From one content area to the next, they are exposed to varied text filled with difficult vocabulary, unfamiliar concepts, and decontextualized language. We hear of the struggles English language learners face across the content areas as they feel overwhelmed with language and content. However, content instruction provides rich opportunities for English language learners to make connections and draw upon personal experiences to support their learning. It offers great opportunities to make instruction applicable and exciting.

Content instruction *is* the world in which our students live: the history of our world and ourselves, the beauty of the arts, the study of our health, and how things work. Such rich content and familiar contexts provide a perfect vehicle for students to develop academic language. This is not to say that it is an easy task for students to navigate language and content simultaneously, but teachers have a rich base from which to plan and facilitate high levels of academic language development.

Language Input

Academic language development is twofold. On one hand, students need to understand the language to access content. This is often thought of as *language input*. Students understand the messages "coming in." In turn, they must be able to share their thinking orally and in writing. This is referred to as *language output*, whereby students use their knowledge of the language and content to share what they have learned. I begin here with a discussion of language input and a variety of strategies teachers can use to facilitate comprehension, followed by a discussion of language output.

To support students' comprehension of language, teachers must create lessons that bring content to life for English language learners. Too often we use language as the sole transmitter of information. We lecture at students and read to them. This provides students with a limited foundation from which to draw meaning. If they are at early stages of second-language acquisition, language alone may not be enough to support comprehension. **Based on the work of Stephen Krashen (1985), we understand that English language learners need comprehensible input for language acquisition to occur.** The content presented to students must be shared in a way that is meaningful. In addition, the input should be at a level slightly above students' current level of proficiency (i+1). The i represents the language-development level students have reached; therefore, the input must be only slightly above that level in order to be understood, represented by the +1. Specially Designed Academic Instruction in English (SDAIE) strategies help students comprehend content by presenting it through rich contexts that make the learning comprehensible. This implies that teachers are knowledgeable about where students are in their content knowledge and language acquisition in order to plan and implement lessons that are at an appropriate level.

Specially Designed Academic Instruction in English

The use of SDAIE strategies support teachers in their efforts to make content-area instruction comprehensible for English language learners. The common understanding among practitioners is that teaching content to English language learners is a challenge when they may not have the content vocabulary or prior knowledge to make meaning. Content instruction involves an ongoing meaning-making process, new information, and abstract concepts. Though it is a challenge, we must ensure that all students are provided access to all content instruction. Therefore, it is our job as teachers to make sure that students understand what it is that they are learning. Some of my most effective SDAIE strategies include Anticipation Guides, Carousel, Jigsaw, and Multimedia Presentations.

Anticipation Guides

The purpose of Anticipation Guides is to generate prior knowledge, set a purpose for reading, and build curiosity. This strategy helps make content comprehensible because it helps develop the schema that students will need to build upon as they begin to read content-area text.

Students are given a series of statements that relate to a theme, concept, or big idea from a selected reading passage. The statements are usually inferential, asking students to share their opinions on each statement. Individually, students decide whether they agree or disagree with each statement, and then discuss their decisions with a partner.

Classroom Connection

Mrs. Tejeda's sixth graders were preparing to read the Ethiopian folktale *Fire on the Mountain*. Prior to reading the text, Mrs. Tejeda distributed an anticipation guide that prompted students to think about the concept of *honor* (see fig. 3.1). Students were instructed to complete the guide independently. They decided whether they agreed or disagreed with the statements provided. After a few minutes, Mrs. Tejeda asked the students to share their Anticipation Guides with partners. The students talked about the statements with which they agreed and disagreed. After a few minutes, Mrs. Tejeda shared the following with the class. "We are going to be reading a folktale together about Hampton Hsai. As we read through the text, I want you to think about your understanding of the word *honor*. In the end, I will ask whether you thought Hampton Hsai was an honorable man, and why or why not." She asked the students to follow along as she read *Fire on the Mountain*.

Fig. 3.1 Anticipation Guide

Anticipation Guide: _Fire on the Mountain_

Part A:

Pre-reading directions: Carefully read statements 1–4 below. Under the "You" heading, put a check (✓) in the agree column if you mostly agree. Put a check (✓) in the disagree column if you mostly disagree. Be prepared to explain why you checked as you did.

	Agree	Disagree
1. An honorable person is someone who stands by his or her word no matter what.		
2. An honorable person is someone who can learn from his mistakes and change his/her mind.		
3. When misunderstandings occur, it is okay for an honorable person to go against his/her original beliefs.		
4. An honorable person is someone who will do whatever he can to keep his "good name" even if his decision is not what he truly believes.		

Part B:

Purpose for reading: Read the Ethiopian folktale *Fire on the Mountain*. As you read, pay special attention to the actions of Hampton. Was Hampton an honorable man? Be prepared to cite examples from the text to support your position.

After reading activity: Grand conversation about the question posed.
Did the discussion help strengthen your position, or did it challenge your thinking and change your mind?

Carousel

The purpose of this strategy is to generate prior knowledge or check for understanding. It involves students working in small groups, allowing peers to serve as scaffolds in language and content for one another.

The teacher begins by selecting a series of subtopics that have been taught (or will be taught) as part of a unit of study. He or she writes the subtopic on the top of a sheet of chart paper (one chart paper for each subtopic). The chart papers are then posted in an organized fashion around the classroom for groups of students to walk to and write on. Students are then arranged into small groups of four or five and each group is provided with a different color marker. Each group is asked to begin at a poster. It is important to have enough posters for the number of groups you have in order to assure participation for all students. Each group writes on their poster everything they can think of or have learned about the subtopic listed on the poster. Allow each group to work on each poster for three minutes. At the teacher's command, students then rotate to the next poster and repeat the process. Groups should not repeat what is already written on the posters. This strategy makes critical thinking increasingly more challenging as groups move from one poster to the next. After groups have had a chance to rotate to all the posters, the teacher takes some time to review what was written on each poster and clarifies any misconceptions.

Jigsaw

This strategy is a reading strategy that helps students reach deeper levels of comprehension for a small segment of text. It develops interdependence since students are responsible to a larger group, and it develops confidence in struggling readers who need to process only a small portion of the text at hand. This strategy supports English language learners because they can process a smaller amount of complex academic language. They then have an opportunity to discuss their thinking with other classmates who read the same part prior to sharing it with the whole class.

The teacher begins by selecting a nonfiction text for students to read. He or she then identifies about five logical stopping points in the text. Usually, separating the text at subheadings helps keep key ideas together. The stopping points are numbered 1–5. Students are then numbered off. The number each student is assigned should correspond to the number of the section that he or she will be responsible for reading. After students have read their assigned sections, students with the same number gather as a group. This creates an expert group within that specific section. Students will then be given the opportunity to discuss the section they read together. This is a good opportunity for struggling readers to check in with their groups to see if they understood the material. In addition, English language learners get a chance to hear their peers talk about the selection (language models), as well as rehearse what they intend to share.

Multimedia Presentations

The purpose of this strategy is to generate prior knowledge through varied sources of information or to present one's learning. Multimedia Presentations present information through multiple sources that can bring content to life through different forms of written and visual media. Some examples include traditional text, pictures, sound, video, graphics, moving images, icons, words, and interaction. Because a lack of prior knowledge inhibits reading comprehension (Lesaux and Kieffer 2010), multimedia can provide students with background knowledge, as well as show students different ways in which people share information. In turn, this strategy is a purposeful way for students to demonstrate their thinking and learning

Academic Language Output

Many of the SDAIE strategies we have learned and use can often be used as ELD strategies as well (refer to Chapter 6). When an instructional strategy is used to help content become comprehensible to students—that is, for students to make meaning of the information—you are presenting SDAIE. When you are using a strategy to provide students with an opportunity to develop academic language—that is, to use language to share what they have learned orally or in writing—it is an ELD strategy. Figure 3.2 demonstrates how integrating strategies can result in making content comprehensible as well as helping students develop academic language.

Fig. 3.2 The Outcome of Incorporating Instructional Strategies

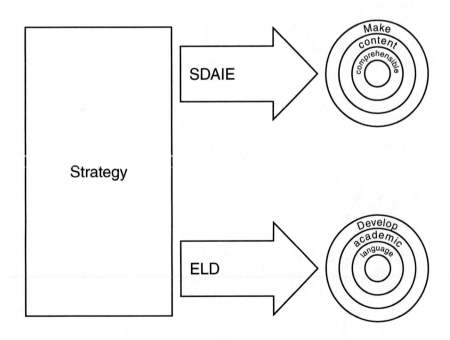

I like to think of ELD as the opportunities we provide for students to hear, practice, and develop academic language. It facilitates academic language development. This includes explicitly providing the vocabulary and functions and forms of language that they will use to share what they have learned and understood through SDAIE strategies. Without the ELD portion, we fail to gain a clear understanding of what students actually understood and learned from the lesson at hand.

Opportunities for comprehensible output are necessary if students are to develop academic language. Students need opportunities to talk about their learning in order to support academic language development. They need to learn how to write about their thinking through different written forms and genres. They need to learn how to share their thinking orally and engage in dialogues and discussions around their learning. Oral and written discourse across the curriculum is just as important as critically comprehending what one reads. To be successful in academia and beyond, we need to develop all aspects of academic language.

Classroom Connection

I can remember my high school Spanish class, sitting with my friends who all became pretty confident in reading and comprehending Spanish. They enjoyed listening to the tapes in class and reading and answering the questions from the dialogues; but when it came to having a conversation in Spanish, they froze. They had acquired language through comprehensible input and felt confident understanding the language. However, they could not speak or write well in Spanish because we rarely had opportunities to use it in real contexts.

If we expect English language learners to become fluent in English and to reach high levels of academic achievement, they must be able to read, write, listen, *and* speak in English. They need multiple, diverse opportunities to use English for academic purposes.

Students are not just learning enough English to engage in a conversation with a friend or within their community but to be able to share their thinking about complex concepts and content in school. Students have to be able to share in English their understanding of big ideas and abstract concepts in critical and creative ways.

Facilitating Thinking

One of the most important lessons I think I have learned as a teacher of academic language development is my role in students' thinking processes. Students are asked to engage in diverse thinking processes across the curriculum. Whether we are asking them to engage in critical thinking, creative thinking, convergent thinking, divergent thinking, inductive thinking, or deductive thinking, our role as a teacher is to guide the thinking process. Too often as teachers, we ask low-level questions that require little to no thinking on the part of the student. The table on page 56, *Thinking Processes*, provides a brief overview of each of the thinking processes.

Thinking Processes

Critical Thinking	Critical thinking involves conceptualizing information and analyzing it in a way that leads to an evaluation of the information; challenging perspectives and points of view are supported with justification. Critical thinking often involves both convergent and divergent thinking.
Creative Thinking	Creative thinking involves creating something new. It can include building upon information and doing something original with it. It builds toward divergent thinking where a new perspective, point of view, or even a new idea is created. Creative thinking typically involves divergent thinking.
Convergent Thinking	Convergent thinking works towards finding the right answer. It is a process of bringing information together to come to a central, sought-out idea or concept as the answer.
Divergent Thinking	Divergent thinking is often thought of as the opposite of convergent thinking. In divergent thinking there may be multiple answers. We start at a core or a problem and think about many possible answers or solutions.
Inductive Thinking	Similar to an educated guess, inductive reasoning is the process of drawing conclusions from a collection of observations. It is moving from specific observations to generalizations. It is similar to a bottoms-up approach, where we build towards an idea based on an observation or noted fact, and though the conclusion may not always be possible, it is grounded in some observation that leads to the conclusion.
Deductive Thinking	Opposite to inductive thinking, deductive thinking starts from the more general and moves to the specific. It begins with a premise that is then narrowed to the point of truth. In math, we use deductive thinking to prove theorems.

Classroom Connection

The students in Mr. Fischer's sixth-grade class had just finished reading a textbook chapter on adaptations. He engaged the students in a grand conversation of the text, asking "Which animals were they talking about?" "How did they adapt?" The students simply looked in their books and found the answers. Mr. Fischer acknowledged the correct answers and then asked the students to close their books and get ready for lunch.

I had a chance to talk with Mr. Fischer about the lesson and the process of thinking in which his students had engaged. After a brief discussion and a critical look at the questions that were asked, he realized that his students were using basic recall thanks to low-level thinking questions. His students were not asked to think, they just had to find the information. These types of questions are considered low-level questions mainly because they do not require students to think beyond the text. The answer to these questions can be found by locating the answer in the book. If we stop at these questions, we have stifled our students' thinking process. Our questions probe the thinking we ask of our students.

As a follow-up to our discussion, Mr. Fischer generated some new questions, including, "Why is it important for an animal to be able to adapt to its environment?" "What type of adaptation might an animal need to survive in the habitat?" "How do you adapt to your environment?" The new questions required students to infer, engage in creative thinking, and move beyond the text to generate an answer. The key is to be mindful of our questioning. Are we asking the kinds of questions that lead to higher-level thinking skills and processes? This question is critical if we are expecting students to become knowledgeable, critical, creative thinkers for the twenty-first century. If we can get students thinking at higher levels, they will in turn be required to talk using more complex language. We will be asking them to practice language functions of inference, justification, evaluation, and critical dialogue. The questions we ask lead to the process of thinking in which we engage students, which in turn requires students to use academic language to share their thinking. The role of questioning is powerful. It directly impacts thinking and the development of academic language.

Conclusion

Academic language includes the complex vocabulary, functions, and forms of language presented across the curriculum. Students need to understand language presented in every content area, and in turn be able to share what they have learned. We want to think about content-area instruction as an opportunity to facilitate academic language development through rich content and authentic, engaging learning opportunities. Through the use of SDAIE strategies, we can help make the content comprehensible for English language learners. Students will then need the language necessary to share what they have learned. Below is an overview of what teachers must think, understand, and employ when facilitating academic language:

- Content is the primary objective.

- Academic language development is a by-product of content knowledge and concept development.

- Academic language development provides opportunities for comprehensible output.

- Academic language development provides opportunities for developing academic language functions, forms, vocabulary, and fluency (ELD).

- Academic language development provides opportunities for interacting with different classmates on a daily basis.

- Systematic building is built upon what students know in the content areas and language.

- Thinking processes connect to language functions.

- As teachers, the questions we ask will guide student thinking and lead to intended language output.

Reflection Questions

1. What does academic language mean to you?

2. How can you make content comprehensible for students?

3. Which materials or strategies have you used to support English language learners in understanding content? Why were they effective?

4. In what ways have you provided your students opportunities to demonstrate their thinking orally and in writing?

5. Look back at a comprehension lesson that you have taught. What kinds of questions did you ask your students? Are there additional ways in which you can engage your students in their thinking about the text?

Creating a Language-Rich Environment

"Learning is a social process that occurs through interpersonal interaction within a cooperative context. Individuals, working together, construct shared understandings and knowledge."

— David Johnson

We often hear of the importance of providing students with a print-rich environment to support literacy development. "A print-rich classroom is one in which children interact with many forms of print including signs, labeled centers, wall stories, word displays, labeled murals, bulletin boards, charts, poems, and other printed materials" (Kadlic and Lesiak 2003). When working with English language learners, we must also think about a language-rich environment. The term *language-rich environment* is more commonly used in the literature on the first-language acquisition of infants. Children who come from homes full of meaningful conversations begin school with a rich vocabulary and strong oral discourse. These early oral-language experiences prepare them for developing traditional literacy skills in school.

English language learners begin school and find themselves once again learning a new language. They will rely on language-rich experiences to support their second-language acquisition as they did in learning a first language. They need to hear language used for a variety of purposes, engage in conversations with different partners, and *see* language. Learning is not accomplished by simply receiving information, but via intelligent inquiry and thought through talk and dialogue (Gibbons 2002; Stabb 1986; Chen and Mora-Flores 2006).

The concept of a language-rich environment may be a bit of a paradigm shift for some educators who are used to more traditional, teacher-centered learning environments. "Teachers dominate talk. Students may ask procedural questions and be procedurally engaged, but they are rarely substantively engaged…Cultivating students' talk is crucial…Articulate student talk is key to inquiry, to collaborative learning and to assimilating knowledge in personally meaningful ways" (Boyd and Rubin 2002, 495). Within teacher-centered contexts, students are not provided ample opportunities to engage in dialogue and discussions with one another. Students are seen as passive recipients of information. This type of instructional context does not support students developing a second language. When working with English language learners, teachers need to devise immersed in a student-centered environment full of rich language opportunities. English language learners need to hear language models from a variety of sources. Teachers, peers, books, videos, and other sources of information can serve as models of language. Students need to be immersed in authentic language tasks that make language comprehensible. They need opportunities to share their thinking with one another and to rehearse oral language for academic purposes.

Building a Classroom Community (Physical Space)

A language-rich environment is not a quiet classroom. It is a classroom where students have opportunities to talk with one another around challenging content and serve as language models for one another. A language-rich classroom has desks organized in a way that allows students to see eye-to-eye and provides spaces where students can come together and talk in larger groups. Figure 4.1 is a picture of a fourth-grade classroom. Students are placed in learning pods of 4–6 students. This allows students visible and audible access to one another. They can discuss their learning through partnership tasks and work as a team from their seats. The flexibility of student interactions is made possible by the room organization. A teacher can quickly transition students from a pair-share to a small group activity without asking students to leave their seats. They have materials available and the space needed to focus on the task. This helps teachers maximize instructional time and avoid long transitions.

Fig. 4.1 Example of a Language-Rich Classroom

Figure 4.2 demonstrates how a fifth-grade teacher uses a large carpet area where the class can come together as an entire classroom community. We do not often see these large communal spaces in

upper-grade and middle-school classrooms. But when possible, I would argue that they are instrumental in supporting language development. Students who feel as if they are part of a community feel safe taking risks and sharing their thinking. They are not afraid to try out language because they understand that errors are part of the learning process. They understand that being part of a community means supporting one another, learning from one another, and celebrating accomplishments. I encourage teachers of all ages to think about how they can provide communal spaces for sharing and learning. Through these large-group meetings, English language learners also have the chance to hear additional language models and practice using English for larger audiences.

Fig. 4.2 Example of a Classroom Community

Peer-to-Peer Interaction

Students take on many roles in school, including that of a novice and that of an expert. On many occasions, peers serve as language models for one another. When working alongside a classmate on a task, English language learners are hearing language. They hear peers at different levels of second-language acquisition and use language in real contexts and around rich content. Through these peer interactions, students develop vocabulary, learn content, and engage in oral discourse. English language learners need opportunities to interact with different peers daily, providing students with diverse language models. If we continue to pair them up with the same person, it can limit the exposure of language that they receive. In addition, students who always serve as language models will not have opportunities to be a novice and develop higher levels of language for themselves. We want all students to have an opportunity to feel like an expert—to feel as if they have something to contribute to the classroom community. Therefore, teachers need to be intentional about how they pair students.

Important to peer-to-peer interaction and community building is knowledge of students' language development. Carefully pairing a student with a classmate who is at a level of language acquisition slightly above his or her own is important. For example, if we pair a student at a pre-production level of second-language acquisition with a native speaker, the level of language input may be too complex for the pre-production student to comprehend and acquire. Additionally, we need to be sure that we mix partnerships often. This gives all students an opportunity to serve as language models and learners. A teacher must further model the interaction. English language learners need to see and hear what it means to engage in a peer discussion. This is a great opportunity to model academic language.

Classroom Connection

As part of a unit on the U.S. Constitution, Mrs. Saunders engaged her students in a pre-reading activity. The students were each given an amendment from the Bill of Rights. Mrs. Saunders shared with the students that they were going to have a chance to talk with their classmates about the amendment that they were provided. This was the students' first look at the Bill of Rights and Mrs. Saunders wanted to hear what their initial understanding of the amendments was. To prepare for the pair-share, she invited a student, Gregory, to come forward so that she could model what a pair-share would sound and look like. Mrs. Saunders asked the young man to stand face-to-face with her. She asked him to look her in the eye when she was talking to him and she did the same. She began, "Gregory, I was given the first amendment: freedom of speech, of the press, and of assembly; right to petition. I believe it means that people in the United States have the right to say what they feel, and to express their opinions and their thoughts without getting in trouble for it. They can do this through the media and can bring people together to talk about issues freely, during an assembly or other public venue. What about you, Gregory? Which amendment do you have and what do you think it means?" Gregory then went on to read his amendment to Mrs. Saunders and shared what he thought it meant. Mrs. Saunders concluded by thanking Gregory and asking him to return to his seat.

Teachers can provide students with language frames to help them initiate a dialogue with their peers, or they can just provide the prompt and allow students to use their own language. However, when generating prior knowledge, I always encourage teachers to allow students to share what they know and bring to the learning experience in both language and content. This provides a great opportunity for teachers to take notes and informally assess students' English as well as what students already know about the content and concepts at hand. Once Mrs. Saunders' students begin talking with one another about their amendment, she will learn a great deal about what they already know about the Bill of Rights. She can then build upon their foundation of knowledge and language.

Teacher as Listener

A language-rich classroom includes knowledge of where students are in their English language development. This includes both formal and informal assessments to determine where English language learners are in their second-language acquisition development. When students interact orally with one another, teachers have the opportunity to listen and learn. We hear the language students are bringing to the task, including vocabulary, forms of language, and oral discourse. This informal assessment of language development provides rich information for teachers to build upon. As a professional developer, I have worked with teachers of classrooms ranging from kindergarten through twelfth grade. As part of my trainings on ELD, I ask teachers to engage in a discussion regarding what they have learned from listening to their English language learners. We talk about the value of informal assessments as strong indicators of what students can do in language. The table on pages 68–69, *Teachers' Perspectives on Second-Language Acquisition*, demonstrates what I have learned from my work with teachers after years of listening to English language learners at each level of second-language acquisition.

Teachers' Perspectives on Second-Language Acquisition

At the Pre-production Level

- Teachers use a lot of scaffolding: attention to sentence structure, Total Physical Response, and visual aids.
- Teachers remember that students are building conceptual understanding and may not have the language to share it. Trust the process; if your lessons are engaging and interactive (i.e., provide opportunities for thought, talk, and interaction) your students are learning.
- As their English develops, students will share their learning.
- Teachers should check for understanding to make sure learning is occurring.
- Teachers provide opportunities for hands-on experiences in which students can see their learning in action.
- Teachers provide opportunities for students to use language (at their level) throughout the day based on comprehensible input.
- Teachers teach chants, choral reading, read-alongs, and share-outs. Also, integrate pair-share opportunities for practicing oral language.

At the Early Production Level

- Teachers integrate precision partnering.
- Teachers structure student activities to allow for all students to talk.
- Teachers diversify interactive activities and assign roles, when applicable. Partnerships are mixed up often.
- Students have a strong command of the language needed for daily routines and school norms.
- Students speak very deliberately. They think before they talk, often in simple sentences or oral bulleting.

At the Speech Emergent Level

- Teachers often provide language frames without listening to the students first and end up explicitly teaching and practicing frames with which students are already familiar.
- Students can talk fluently with their friends.
- Students can share what they are doing during an activity, but not always what they are thinking and learning.
- Students are confident during an informal pair-share.
- Visuals of concrete terms help students understand vocabulary.
- Cloze activities, containing sentences with a missing term and a word bank (teachers provide the words to fill in the blank), help students strategically complete a comprehension task. Without the word bank, they may not have the vocabulary needed to fill in the blanks.
- Students are confident in generating questions about their learning.
- Teachers make language a purposeful part of all content areas.
- Teachers should not lose sight of the socio-cognitive framework (Thought, Talk, and Interaction).

Teachers' Perspectives on Second Language Acquisition *(cont.)*

At the Early Advanced Level
• Students sound very fluent, but may still lack the academic language needed to comprehend and share their thinking across the curriculum.   • Teachers provide higher-level language as an example for students to use when talking and writing.   • Students may sound fluent in listening and speaking, but they might have gaps in expressing deeper conceptual understandings and in writing complex and varied types of texts.   • Students need strategies that allow them to use language for expressing higher-level thinking. This includes opportunities for dialogue and opportunities to challenge one another in their thinking and learning.

At the Advanced Level
• Students need to be exposed to different types of texts.   • Students should be writing across different genres, and they should be engaging in creative writing.   • Teachers should engage students in activities in which they use language for a variety of purposes and in front of different audiences (e.g., oral presentations, research reports).   • Students need to think across texts and be engaged in critical thinking. They need to sift, sort, eliminate, validate, and evaluate sources of information, as well as be able to defend their decisions orally and in writing.

Knowledge of students' second-language acquisition provides the basis for teachers to serve as language models and extend students' language. If we do not take the time to listen to our students and to take note of the academic language (vocabulary, functions, forms, and fluency) students use, then we may be modeling language that they already possess. If we listen to their language, we can provide them the next layer in academic language development. For example, if we hear our students say, "The character in the story was brave," we should now be modeling words such as, "The character was valiant because his actions led to helping others." Teachers need to model academic language that will build toward native-like fluency and beyond. This includes allowing and encouraging students to talk progressively more while the teacher talks progressively less.

Low Risk, High Success Contexts

A language-rich environment encourages risk taking. Students need to believe that the class is working together as a language community. In their discussion of the affective-filter hypothesis, Krashen and Terrell (1983) remind us that students need to feel safe when trying out language. They need to know that if they make a mistake, they will not be ridiculed. English language learners need to feel successful as language learners and build their confidence as speakers of English.

Classroom Connection

Mr. Mason's kindergarten class was working on a visual art lesson called *Telling a Story Through Pictures*. The students created art pieces about a special day they spent with their families. Mr. Mason shared with the class that they were going to engage in a gallery walk of everyone's pictures. He posted the pictures all around the classroom. With partners, the students were to walk around the room and share with their partners what they saw in the pictures. They were instructed to use appropriate art vocabulary regarding color, shape, and form. One partnership, Sara and Aidan, had stopped in front of one of the pictures that looked like a family playing at the park. Sara pulled Aidan toward the picture and said, "You go first, or I go first. OK, I see red, I see green. You, you go now." Aidan seemed very timid. With his head slightly down, he looked up at the picture and just nodded in agreement. Sara repeated, "You go." Aidan lifted his head and looked at the picture again. Sara insisted, "Go, Aidan, your turn. It's okay, you can say red and green, too. We can say the same thing together if you want." Aidan looked up again and whispered, "Green, red." Sara excitedly said, "Yes! I see green and red, too. See Aidan—you are so smart. I see green and red, too." Aidan looked up at the picture again and said, "I see people in the picture. The small one is colored in blue with a red shirt." Mr. Mason said, "Great, Aidan! You see the different colors the artist used for pieces of clothing." Aidan's face lit up. He picked his head up and followed Sara to the next picture.

The more confident Aidan felt in sharing his ideas, the more language he used to express his thinking. His fluency improved and he shared longer stretches of language. This was possible through the encouragement of a peer and the reinforcement of the teacher. In turn, Aidan went from a novice to a model of language for Sara. Peer interaction helps English language learners feel comfortable trying out language in a small, intimate context.

Interactive Read-Alouds

Interactive read-alouds are an important component of every classroom. During an interactive read-aloud, the teacher invites students to interact with text. Different from a normal read-aloud, the teacher has a clear objective for the read-aloud and provides opportunities during the reading for students to contribute their thinking. The teacher plans intentional stopping points in the text to check for understanding. The teacher can also call on a few students to share what they understood about the text or engage students in a pair-share.

Classroom Connection

Mr. Reyes's class was reading the chapter titled "Eleven" from *The House on Mango Street* by Sandra Cisneros. After reading only the first paragraph, he stopped and said, "What does this mean to you: 'You open your eyes and everything's just like yesterday, only it's today. And you don't feel eleven at all. You feel like you're still ten.' Why do you think the character would say that? Turn to the person sitting next to you and discuss."

One partnership shared, "I think it means you were just ten the day before so it takes time to feel older. Maybe she means that until you actually have your party and everybody sees you are now eleven then you feel eleven." Mr. Reyes stopped the pair-share after two minutes and asked a few students to share their thinking with the whole class. Then he continued reading and stopping along the way. All the while, students continued to share their comprehension and helped one another to stay on task.

The key in supporting students' listening comprehension is to chunk the text. This allows English language learners to process shorter bits of language at a time. In addition, talking with a peer offers a low-anxiety context for practicing oral language and facilitating comprehension. For English language learners, it provides students with contextualized language. They see how vocabulary and written discourse is used and organized.

Daily Shared-Reading Opportunities

Students need further opportunities to see language. A shared-reading experience differs from a read-aloud because students have visible access to the text being read. For young students, this can happen with a big book or large charts of text. For older readers, teachers can use multiple copies of text or display the text on a document camera or overhead. A shared-reading experience allows students to see the words in print as the teacher reads them. It takes the language-learning experience further as students make sense from oral *and* written language. In addition, similar to a read-aloud, frequent checks for understanding are important in a shared-reading experience. Figures 4.3 and 4.4 on the following page provide pictures of a shared-reading experience in second and fifth grade. You can see from the pictures that students are not only listening to the story, but also following along as the teacher reads the text. Their eyes are on the text as the teacher reads. During a read-aloud, students are usually relying on frequent glimpses of the illustrations. In the case of older students, the class may need to rely completely on listening to the story when no illustrations are available.

Fig. 4.3 Second-Grade Shared-Reading Experience

Fig. 4.4 Fifth-Grade Shared-Reading Experience

Words Introduced Orally and in Context

Word walls are a great resource to support students' reading and writing. Content word walls help students to recall important words in order to comprehend text across the curriculum. These word walls are most effective when students can connect meaning to the words. For example, the teacher can provide pictures, full sentences that use the word, or full texts with the words underlined.

Figures 4.5 and 4.6 below show examples of different word walls.

Fig. 4.5 Example of a Word Wall

Fig. 4.6 Example of a Math Word Wall

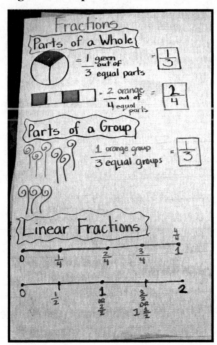

In addition, English language learners need to hear words used naturally throughout the day. In their article, "Deconstructing Language for English Learners," Girard and Spycher (2007) discuss the importance of teachers using precise language and providing students with opportunities to construct and deconstruct language. This includes teacher think-alouds where they model language for students and use the academic language they expect their students to develop.

Classroom Connection

As part of a read-aloud, I had shared the word *eager* with students. I talked with them about the meaning of the word, emphasizing it was a word to which they could relate because I saw them experience it every day. I explained, "Every day when we finish our writer's workshop, you all get very excited, you pick up quickly and show me that you are ready to go out to lunch. I see how *eager* you are to go to lunch. You can't wait." Students began using the word, "I get *eager* for my birthday. I can't wait." "I am *eager* to go to lunch today, too." We continued to read the story and wrapped up our lesson. As the day went on, I was intentional about my language and used the word *eager* when applicable. Eventually I noticed the students using it instead of the phrase, "I can't wait." Though there are other meanings and uses, the purposeful and intentional use of precise language led to students learning and using a new vocabulary word.

Hearing words used in authentic contexts supports students' receptive and expressive vocabulary. We want English language learners to understand the words they hear and, in turn use the words when speaking and writing.

Abundant Classroom Library

The classroom library serves as a valuable resource for English language learners. Through books, students are exposed to large amounts of language. As they read a variety of text across genres and content areas, English language learners are exposed to vocabulary in context. They see how the English language is structured and learn new forms of language. In addition, important to any library is a range of text types. Students need access to a variety of texts, including trade books, magazines, chapter books, newspapers, Web resources, pamphlets, brochures, and other print materials. *Access* means having the reading materials available for students to read in class, take home, and reference throughout the school day. Providing multiple sources of texts helps students access information in different ways. They also see that knowledge can be presented through a variety of print media. As a result, they come across different forms of written discourse. Figures 4.7 and 4.8 provide some examples of how teachers organize their abundant classroom libraries.

Fig. 4.7 Example of a Classroom Library

Fig. 4.8 Example of a Classroom Library

Explicit Language Environment

A language-rich classroom has clear representations of vocabulary and language forms. Modeling proper written language supports English language learners when speaking and writing in English. This includes documenting language forms that students use for a particular function of language and posting it. For example, a third-grade class had been studying animal habitats. They were each asked to orally describe a picture of a desert to their partners and share their wonderings about their pictures. The teacher walked around the room and recorded language forms students had used for description. "I see dry plants. There is a lot of sand. I see a lizard and some rocks. The desert is hot and dry." These language forms were common from most of the students. The teacher then posted the language forms and added a few new ones. Figure 4.9 on the following page presents the language starters the teacher shared and taught the students. The forms then served as a resource for students for future oral and written tasks.

Fig. 4.9 Example of Language Forms

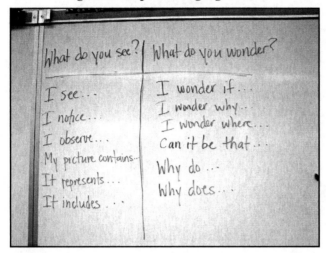

Conclusion

The key in creating a language-rich environment is to immerse students in language. From talking to peers, to seeing examples of language around the room and in varied forms of text, English language learners need to be highly exposed to language. They need daily opportunities to practice using the language that surrounds them. The table below captures what it means to provide English language learners with a language-rich classroom that supports second-language acquisition and academic language development.

How to Build a Language-Rich Classroom

- Create spaces for peer-to-peer interaction using small-group and whole-group settings.
- Encourage peer-to-peer interactions.
- Listen to the language and knowledge students bring to the learning experience.
- Incorporate interactive read-alouds.
- Provide daily shared-reading opportunities.
- Introduce words orally and in print.
- Have an abundant classroom library.
- Encourage daily opportunities to read independently.
- Create an explicit language environment.

Reflection Questions

1. How can you set up your classroom to provide students access to their peers?

2. What opportunities do you provide for your students to talk with different peers daily?

3. How do you listen and take note of the vocabulary words and forms of language your students use when engaging in a task? In what way? What do you do with the information once you have gathered it?

4. How do you use knowledge of your students' current level of language acquisition to guide your own language use and plan explicit academic language instruction?

Literacy Instruction for English Language Learners: Essential Elements

"It is not enough to simply teach children to read; we have to give them something worth reading. Something that will stretch their imaginations—something that will help them make sense of their own lives and encourage them to reach out toward people whose lives are quite different from their own."

— Katherine Patterson

As facilitators of literacy, teachers should expect their students to become critical and creative thinkers—thinkers who can decipher credible sources of information, challenge text, and express their thoughts and opinions with justification, both orally and in writing. Too often in the education of English language learners, the expectations for literacy include developing foundational skills such as phonemic awareness, phonics, and basic levels of comprehension. These skills are important in the development of all students, and a good reader will use them to think deeply about text and make decisions. However, they are not an end to the process, but a foundation upon which to build. There is a misconception that English language learners cannot think deeply about text because they have not developed sufficient English to make sense of what they read. There is a misconception that English language learners should wait until they have reached conversational levels of proficiency before teaching them to be strategic, thoughtful readers. There is a misconception that English language learners are not capable of thinking and learning at a level comparable to their English proficient peers. These misconceptions are not only false, but research and practice have shown us that English language learners, with the proper support, can reach high levels of English literacy comparable to, or higher than, their English-dominant peers (Goldenberg 2008).

The research on second-language literacy development has demonstrated time and time again that the optimal learning conditions for developing English literacy is through the use of the primary language (L1) (Goldenberg 2008). Students who learn to read in a primary language can transfer their learned skills, strategies, and conceptual knowledge to learning to read in English. They use their knowledge of letters and sounds to decode words when reading and writing. They can draw upon their knowledge of words to figure out the meaning of text when letters and sounds get in the way. Teachers can teach them comprehension strategies to work through text challenges, and skills to process information fluidly. Students write across genres and develop written discourse and knowledge of syntax. These skills are not relearned when developing second-language literacy; rather, they are recalled and then applied to reading in English. What teachers need to understand, however, is that this transfer may not always be automatic or natural for students. English language learners with strong L1 literacy skills need to be made aware of the transferable skills and knowledge from their L1 to English (Goldenberg 2010). This includes knowledge of cognates, knowledge of letter-sound connections that are similar in both languages, knowledge of syntactic similarities and gaps, and knowledge of word meanings.

The transfer of language knowledge must be made explicit for students. I share a few of these here: cognates and letter-sound connections, and then I move toward discussing the essential elements of literacy in English in the absence of primary language support. These include the role of oral language, phonemic awareness and phonics, written discourse, and vocabulary reading comprehension.

Cognates

Cognates are words that have similar spelling, meaning and pronunciation from one language to another. The similarities between the Spanish and English languages offer a large number of cognates for Spanish-speaking English language learners to draw upon when making meaning from words. The challenge occurs, however, when students have not developed enough strong primary-language (L1) vocabulary upon which to rely in order to understand the English cognates. Many academic words we see across the content areas have Spanish-English cognates, but if students are not familiar with the word and its meaning in Spanish, it will not support English language development. For example, in social studies the word *federation* shares the Spanish cognate *federación*, the French *fédération*, and the Italian *federazione*. However, if students do not know the word or meaning of *federation* in their primary language, their L1 vocabulary does not support their learning the word *federation*. The development of a primary language helps facilitate second-language literacy.

There are also a large number of cognates that are familiar to English language learners even without primary language instruction to facilitate reading in a second language. For example, the word *family* in Italian is *famiglia*, and in German, *familie*. Such common, everyday concepts and terms help students make meaning when learning to read in English. But again, teachers need to make explicit the transfer of words from one language to another. I remember one summer when I was presenting professional development on developing academic language, specifically the use of cognates, a participant asked, "What if I don't know Spanish? How can I share cognates with my students?" Students are active participants in their learning. You can ask the students themselves, "Is there a word you know that sounds similar in another language? Can you share that with us? What does the word mean in your language?" This is a very empowering process for English language learners. They get excited to share their knowledge of their primary language. They feel smart; they know something many others may not. You will also find that students will talk to one another. They will confirm, add to, or sometimes correct one another if a cognate is correct or incorrect.

False cognates are words that look similar, sound similar, and are pronounced similarly from one language to another, yet they have different meanings. For example, the words *pie* in English and *pie* in Spanish are false cognates because *pie*—though in both languages is spelled the same and sounds similar—means "foot" in Spanish but "pastry" in English. You will find that English language learners feel empowered as the vocabulary experts, while we, the novices learn alongside them.

Additionally, I always encourage my teachers to maximize the use of their resources. There are great cognate lists available on the Internet. Many of these lists include cognates and false cognates. Also, refer to the cognates in the Appendix on pages 145–151. It is a great way for teachers to plan ahead and identify cognates for key vocabulary that they may be teaching in English.

Letter-Sound Connections

The transfer of phonics—or letter-sound connections—from one language to another depends upon the two languages. For students who have learned to read in Spanish, there is a strong letter-sound connection to English. The alphabet is similar with the exception of the additional letters *ch*, *rr*, *ll*, and *ñ* for the Spanish language. Moreover, the sounds of letters from one language have very similar sounds to another language. There are exceptions, as the English language has many complex, unique sound-spelling patterns not found in Spanish. For example, some exceptions in English include dipthongs (e.g., *oi*, *oy*), digraphs (e.g., *ng*, *th*, *sh*, *tch*), or r-controlled sounds (e.g., *er*, *ir*, *ur*, *ar*) to name a few. Though there may be slight differences in the letter-sound patterns from Spanish to English, there are many more similarities, and the process of using phonics to decode words and understand them varies. In either language, students must learn how to "read" the sounds the letters make in order to form words. This is a discrete language skill that transfers from Spanish to English. Yet again, teachers need to be explicit in pointing out the similarities and sharing the similar decoding process. One resource that I have used to improve my own knowledge of similarities and differences across languages is *Words Their Way with English Learners: Word Study for Spelling, Phonics, and Vocabulary Instruction* by Donald Bear et. al (2006). This book provides the transfer skills from many languages to English. We need to continue to learn as much as we can to support English language learners who own strong primary-language literacy skills and explicitly share how to transfer these skills to English.

For many English language learners across the country, learning to read in a primary language has not been the norm. "Fewer than one-quarter of elementary-age English language learners and less than half of secondary-age English language learners are foreign-born" (Capps et. al 2005, Goldenberg 2010). In the absence of bilingual education programs, these students do not have the opportunity to develop strong first-language literacy skills. Therefore, they cannot rely on the transfer of such skills when learning to read in English. These students begin school in kindergarten with the dual task of developing English and literacy in English. For these students, we need to provide additional support to meet their needs. As teachers of English language learners in English-speaking settings, we have to begin by believing that this task is possible. We need to begin the year expecting that all of our students will reach high levels of English literacy. An environment of high expectations coupled with the right instructional scaffolds will make this possible.

Developing literacy in a second language is similar to developing literacy in a primary language. As mentioned earlier, many of the conceptual processes among languages are similar and can transfer from one language to another. Successful practices in developing second language literacy include developing oral language and explicit instruction in phonemic awareness, phonics, vocabulary development, morphology, comprehension strategies, and written discourse. **The *what* students need to learn does not change, it is the *how* we teach that can further support English language learners.** I share some of my most effective strategies for supporting English learners in developing the skills needed for literacy.

Developing Oral Language

Oral language facilitates English literacy development (Saunders and O'Brien 2006, Geva 2006). Students learn to use the sounds and words that they have used while engaging in oral conversations to try to make sense of text. They recall vocabulary that they are familiar with and begin reading stories by simply "reading" the pictures. When they begin learning letters and sounds, they connect them to words and sounds they use when speaking. Critical to English language learners, second-language literacy development is the development of English. However, as Goldenberg (2010) stated, English language learners do not need to develop a high level of English to begin to learn to read in English. English language learners are very successful at developing the discrete skills such as phonemic awareness and phonics in English while developing oral language in English.

Strategies for Developing Oral Language

At this point, I would like to share some strategies for developing oral language, followed by a discussion on how to support English language learners in phonemic awareness and phonics. The goal is to give students ample opportunities to hear what model English sounds like, to practice speaking in English, and to engage in authentic oral discourse with diverse peers.

Student-Teacher Talk

The teacher serves a key role in the development of language and literacy for English language learners. For most children, their teacher is the main model of English. Teachers need to be mindful of their talk and speak clearly and intentionally. You want to be specific in your talk and establish routines where students will hear common academic language frequently. This includes using precise language when giving students directions. For example, instead of saying, "Give it to me," you can say, "Please hand me the book about animals that is on my desk." We must be intentional and explicit. We cannot assume that English language learners are already equipped with common, everyday jargon. They are in the process of trying to comprehend what is being said while learning how to express their needs, wants, and learning. We are models of language: the sounds of language, the structure of the language, semantics, and oral discourse. The methods I recommend later in this chapter offer teachers an opportunity to interact with students in whole group, small groups, and individually; demonstrate diverse contexts in which language is used; and expose students to different forms of oral discourse.

Pair-Share

In chapter 2, I mentioned the importance of students engaging in conversations with one another. Pair-Share is a simple strategy for engaging students in talking. Students are asked to talk with a partner about the task at hand. Whether structured or impromptu, the purpose is to give students an opportunity to practice speaking in English. When structured, the teacher should identify what and when in the lesson he or she wants students to engage in a pair-share. The teacher can also provide sentence frames that students can use to begin their discussions with their peers. I would not encourage providing sentence frames too often for a pair-share because students should be working on developing oral-language fluency.

Teachers want students to be able to engage in a free flow of ideas and not worry about language. Teachers want students to bring what they know in language and content to the pair-share. It is a friendly exchange of both language and content, and students will naturally acquire language during the exchange. When the lesson has a clear language objective and the teacher is teaching particular language functions and forms, I would suggest using the sentence frame. It is important for students to feel successful as language users and to provide them with the opportunity to use language in a natural environment, such as a pair-share.

Classroom Connection

During a math lesson on ratio and proportion, Ms. Fuentes read to her students the book *If You Hopped Like a Frog* by David Schwartz. She read, "If you hopped like a frog...you could jump from home plate to first base in one leap!" The students' faces were in awe at the illustration of a young boy leaping to first base. Ms. Fuentes asked, "How is this possible? What does this mean to you? Turn and talk, tell your partner what this first idea means to you." Students quickly turned to the person sitting next to them. It was apparent that the students were used to Pair-Sharing because they already knew with whom to share. There was no lag time in students looking for partners. Some students shared, "I think it means that a frog can jump pretty far, and even though they are small, they have strong legs. So if we had legs like frogs—really strong and long—then we could jump better." His partner agreed, "Yup, and we could do a lot more, too. We could jump over fences and across the street easier. It's pretty cool all the things we could do if we did jump like a frog." Ms. Fuentes directed the students to turn back to the book and she continued reading. She stopped often and asked students to Pair-Share while she listened to their thinking. After each pair-share Ms. Fuentes would either ask students to share what they discussed or she would tell the class what she heard them talking about. After she finished reading the book, she showed students an interesting feature of the book. In the back, the author provided all of the mathematical computations that explained the ratios presented throughout the book. She took the time to review the math problems. By doing this, she was able to make connections to what she heard students share during their pair-shares to help them comprehend ratio and proportions.

A Pair-Share can serve as an informal assessment. When I want to do a quick check for understanding, I often ask students to share their thinking with partners. This allows me the opportunity to hear what students have understood from the lesson and to listen to their English. I monitor for language and learning. For example, if I ask students to discuss what we learned about the difference between mammals and reptiles, I listen for their knowledge of the content. I can focus on the vocabulary they select, which animals they mention, what they know about those animals, and how they understand in which group they belong. In addition, I can listen for the language they use when comparing the two. Are they saying, "A dolphin is a mammal" and "A lizard is a reptile?" Or are they using more elaborate language for comparisons, such as, "A dolphin is a mammal, whereas a lizard is a reptile." By listening to students' discussions, teachers can incorporate the language they already understand within future lessons.

Table Talk

A larger context for sharing language and learning is a Table Talk. Similar to a Pair-Share, these can be structured or impromptu. In a Table Talk, if your classroom is organized in a way where students sit in learning pods (groups of students at a table), they can easily talk with one another. They see eye-to-eye and are close enough to hear each other. It makes a table talk quick and simple because students do not have to move around. The teacher can have students work at the table on a structured activity and set language objectives where they talk for a given purpose. The teacher can give students a chance to check in with their table frequently through impromptu table talks. During lessons, the teacher can stop and ask students at a table to talk briefly about what has been taught. This gives the teacher a chance to check in, walk around, and listen to what students are saying. It gives English language learners a chance to check in with their peers and see if they are following along. It also gives those English language learners who are not quite ready for a pair-share the opportunity to listen to their table peers as they share their thinking and language.

Both pair-share and table talk are equally important because students serve as language models and learners, and are learning how to engage in oral discourse.

Find Someone Who...

This activity asks students to mingle with classmates to try to find someone who fits the different descriptions or abilities listed on their worksheets. This activity helps students to get to know their classmates as they work on developing oral language. Typically the activity provides statements such as, "Find someone who..." or "Find someone who can..." Students then approach their peers and say, "Can you...?" or "Do you know...?" For English language learners, I like to provide the language they will use when asking their peers the question. So instead of writing, "Find someone who..." on the sheet, I write the question they would ask their peers. English language learners do not need to convert the statement into a question; it gives them the language to complete the task. This helps them focus on comprehension and fluency of language as opposed to struggling with the task. It allows students to engage in the activity without letting language get in the way of their success. In turn, they hear, practice, and develop their English language skills.

To begin the activity, it is helpful to first model it for students. I ask a student volunteer to help me demonstrate how to use the worksheet and talk to his or her peers. I explain that the volunteer will walk up to a classmate and read the classmate a question on the worksheet. If the peer can answer *yes* to the question, the volunteer writes his or her name in the box. I explain to students that the person who signs his or her name in the square will have to demonstrate the skill to the class, so he or she has to be honest. Allow students 5–10 minutes to complete the activity or until a student has filled in all of the boxes. The questions can also be tailored to content-area topics. An example of a template of what this activity looks like is provided on page 92.

Find Someone Who…

Can name a mammal. List the mammal named. _____ _____ _____ Name: _____	Owns a reptile. List the reptile that he or she owns. _____ Name: _____	Can name three amphibians. List the amphibians named. _____ _____ _____ Name: _____
Knows what *viviparous* means. Write the definition. _____ _____ _____ Name: _____	Has been to the zoo. List three animals he or she saw at the zoo. _____ _____ _____ Name: _____	Can identify two classifications of animals. List the two classifications. _____ _____ _____ Name: _____
Can explain the difference between an African elephant and an Asian elephant? Write the explanation. _____ _____ _____ Name: _____	Can name three reptiles. List the reptiles named. _____ _____ _____ Name: _____	Can name a pet that he or she owns and the classification it belongs in. List the animal and classification. _____ _____ _____ Name: _____

Phonemic Awareness and Phonics

Discrete literacy skills, including knowledge of the sounds and symbols of a language, are integral to literacy development. Research has shown that English language learners are able to develop discrete literacy skills at a level comparable to English dominant students while also developing their English oral language. This includes developing phonemic awareness and phonics.

Phonemic awareness is knowledge of the sounds of a language and the ability to manipulate those sounds to produce words. Phonemic awareness is an exclusively oral exercise, in which students are learning to listen for the sounds of the English language. This includes the sounds that letters make when spoken. Phonemic awareness has shown to be a strong predictor of early reading success (Adams 1990). When students are able to listen for, identify, isolate, and combine sounds, they will be better able to read the symbols (letters) that represent those sounds. When students are taught to use their knowledge of phonemic awareness (sounds of a language) to read letters, they are developing phonics skills: they can identify the letter they are seeing and make the sound that is connected to the letter or letter pattern.

Phonics instruction includes teaching students the letters of the alphabet and the letter combinations that stand for sounds in English. We teach students phonics to use when decoding words. Students sound out words in order to read them. This is just one way in which a child might process text to read. Alone, phonics does not develop proficient readers. The cognitive process of understanding the concept of phonics, rather, is key. Students need to understand that text is created by letters and sounds put together to create words. Words are then joined together to tell stories and provide information. This is a foundation of reading, and when taught explicitly, can support English language learners who are learning to read in a second language. A caution to teachers of English language learners is that this is only one piece to the complex process of learning to read. English language learners should not be reduced to relying too much on phonics without understanding that the real purpose of reading is for meaning. They need a holistic reading program that not only includes phonics, but that also provides instruction in reading comprehension, vocabulary, oral language development, morphology, and writing. Together, these skills lead to second-language literacy development.

There are a variety of ways in which teachers approach the teaching of phonemic awareness and phonics. I believe the debate is not whether we should teach phonics or not, but how we should teach it to English language learners, and how we make it part of a holistic program.

Strategies for Teaching Phonics

Here are a few strategies that I have used to teach phonics, including Word Building, Word Families, and Letter-Sound Collage.

Word Building

In a Word Building activity, the teacher engages students in a part-to-whole approach for teaching phonics. This is also called a *synthetic approach*. In word building, teachers sound out words with students one letter at a time. Students are asked to focus on the individual letters and the sounds that they make and blend the sounds together. This is typically done with words that contain common phonics patterns so students can practice the letter-sound combination. Providing a visual can further support English language learners in the process of reading.

Word Families

Important to teaching phonics is a diversity of approaches. Some students may learn best from a part-to-whole approach, while others need a more holistic word-learning approach. With this strategy, we take words as a whole and find patterns in the words. This is often referred to as a *whole-to-part* or *analytic approach*. In Word Families, I usually begin by pulling words from a text that I have read with students. I select words that have a similar letter-sound pattern to analyze with the students. For example, if I display the words *ring*, *king*, *sing*, and *thing*, I would ask the students to look at the words carefully and identify any similarities among the words. Students identify the letters *-ing* or *-ng*. The digraph is actually /ng/ which is a part of words such as *sang* and *hung* as well. We would then use the letters *-ing* with students to create a family of words. The important thing is that students understand the concept of looking for patterns in words and, in turn, are learning the letter-sound combinations. In addition, students can then use their knowledge of the pattern to read other words that contain the same patterns. Once students have identified the pattern, teachers can explicitly talk about the sounds of the pattern they identified. Students can then think about other words they know that contain the pattern. Attaching an image or example to the words as a visual can provide added support for English language learners.

Letter-Sound Collage

Letter-Sound Collages were always engaging for my students. Working in small groups, students are assigned a letter-sound pattern. Teachers then provide all groups with many different sources of print that contain pictures (e.g., newspapers, magazines, brochures, catalogues) as well as scissors, glue, and a large sheet of paper. As a group, students find any pictures of items, ideas, or themes that contain their assigned letter-sound pattern. Students enjoy collaborating and working together, searching for examples that depict their letter-sound pattern and creating their group collage. Ideally, when students are finished with their collages, they are encouraged to share their findings. Figures 5.1 and 5.2 on the following page are examples of Letter-Sound Collages created by fifth-grade students at varying levels of second-language acquisition. One collage has students looking for images representing the long /ā/ sound and images representing the suffix *-tion*. Within the same activity all students feel successful at their levels.

Figure 5.3 on page 97 offers a look at students engaged in the development of their collages. It is an enjoyable, creative, and a collaborative experience for students.

Fig. 5.1 Example of Letter-Sound Collage for the /ā/ Sound

Fig. 5.2 Example of Letter-Sound Collage for the Suffix -tion

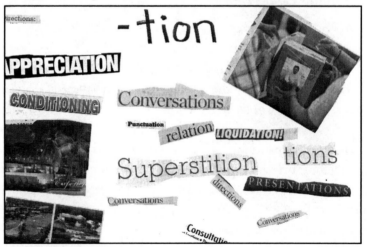

Fig. 5.3 Students Working Together Creating Their Letter-Sound Collages

Phonics Carousel

Another purposeful activity for students is the Phonics Carousel. The teacher begins by selecting at least six sound-spelling patterns that students have previously learned. On large sheets of chart paper, the teacher writes one letter-sound pattern on the top of each sheet. Students are then placed into small groups of three or four and given a different color marker. Students within each group then assign a scribe and stand next to one of the posters. Once students are in place (one group per chart), they are instructed to write all of the words the group can think of that contain the letter-pattern written on the chart paper in front of them. After a few minutes, students are directed to rotate to the next chart. The process is repeated, but students should not repeat any words that are currently on the chart paper. This strategy helps students familiarize themselves with words that they may not know and to practice reading the letter-sound pattern. Once all of the groups have rotated to each poster, it is time to stop the carousel. I then ask one member of each group to bring a chart to the front of the classroom, so we review the words as a class. What I found most effective for English language learners was the opportunity to work as a team and to be able to practice reading words in English.

These opportunities help students develop their oral language and phonics skills, and they provide students with a comfortable environment in which students are able to take risks with the sounds of the English language within a small group of peers.

Vocabulary Instruction

Vocabulary has a strong connection to reading comprehension. Along with teaching students the discrete skill of phonics and phonemic awareness is building their vocabularies to make meaning when reading. The more words students know, the more strategic they can be as readers. Many students rely on their knowledge of words to make sense of text. When phonics can only take them as far as simple decodable words, students will intentionally use their knowledge of words and their meanings to read words.

Classroom Connection

Stephanie was fluently reading through her history textbook when she came across the word *controversial*. She attempted to read the word using her knowledge of phonics. She read *cont-* and then stopped. She took her eyes off the text and started thinking about words she knew that began with *cont-*. She said, "Contract, continent, contact, controversy." She reread the text and when she came to the word *controversial* again, she was able to read through it.

In the example on the previous page, Stephanie used her knowledge of phonics coupled with her knowledge of words and their meaning to read the text. She knew which word was right because it made sense in the text. Students should be encouraged to bring together their knowledge of words with phonics when reading. This is an effective skill demonstrating how important it is to develop students' English oral language and vocabulary.

Most words that students know and use when listening, speaking, reading, and writing are learned through incidental exposure to words. For example, when students engage in conversations with others, listen to the radio, watch television, browse the Internet, and read a variety of texts, they are exposed to words in context. Meaningful, frequent exposure to words in context facilitates vocabulary development. Anderson and Nagy (1992) explain that only about 10% of words students learn in a year are taught through explicit vocabulary instruction in school. The remaining 90% come from incidental, informal experiences with language. With this in mind, teachers need to be mindful of the amount and utility of words they choose to teach during vocabulary-instruction time.

When explicitly teaching vocabulary, teachers need to be strategic about which words to focus on. You want to identify a small number of words, approximately 8–10 per week, that are used for focused vocabulary instruction. These words should be high-utility words that students will have opportunities to use often and across the curriculum to help develop their receptive and expressive vocabulary. They need to understand the words and also know how to use them when speaking and writing. This includes providing plenty of opportunities for students to use the words in context.

Strategies for Teaching Vocabulary

Explicit vocabulary instruction should involve diverse encounters with words. I have seen teachers use thoughtfully created graphic organizers that ask students to define the word, identify a synonym and antonym, use the word in a sentence, provide a visual and give an example. These are great, but should not be the only tools we use to engage students with words. When learning words, students need to use them. They need to be invested in learning the words and have opportunities to play with words. Some strategies I have used include Vocabulary Self-Selection (VSS), Where in the World?, and Morphology.

Vocabulary Self-Selection

The Vocabulary Self-Selection strategy developed by Martha Haggard (1982) is a research-based vocabulary practice for all students. I have modified it a bit in my work with English language learners to include the following steps:

1. Working independently, have students identify five words from a unit with which they are unfamiliar or would like to further explore.

2. Tell students that they will research their five words, including the definition, part of speech, and a visual representation. (This is typically done for homework on index cards.)

3. Place students in groups of three or four. Ask students to take turns sharing their words.

4. After students have shared their words, ask each group to work together in identifying five words that they would like to share with the class for further study.

5. The teacher lists the five words selected from each group. As a class, they now negotiate and decide collectively which ten words they would like to explore as a class.

6. The teacher uses the final word list to engage the class in additional vocabulary strategies throughout the week.

What makes this strategy most effective is the role of your students. Students are more invested in learning the words because they select the words themselves. Even though many of the original words selected by the students may not end up in the final class list, students have already taken time to learn their own words. Students also learn how to work together and negotiate with one another to make communal decisions.

Where in the World?

Developing communicative competence, understanding, and appropriate word usage across contexts are important skills in vocabulary development. With these skills, students are asked to think about their vocabulary words in context. Instead of using the ineffective practice of just defining words and using them in a sentence, students are asked to identify where, when, and how the words are used in the real world. Students are given the task of being mindful of the language used in their surroundings. For one week, they record in their notebooks when they hear or see the vocabulary words used in the world around them. This can include cutting out full sentences or articles where the word is contained, writing down an example of a conversation they heard, or writing their own examples of how the word can be used. Where in the World? allows students to see how their vocabulary words are used in real-world contexts. The goal of this strategy is for students to learn to use the words in similar contexts themselves and to make the words part of their expressive vocabulary. This conscious focus of the language students hear and see around them supports their language development.

Morphology

Morphemes are the smallest unit of meaning in a language. Morphemes are put together to form words. Morphology includes teaching students about prefixes, suffixes, root words, and base words. The table on the following page provides an overview of the terminology associated with morphology.

Morphology

Base Words	A free morpheme that stands alone as a word.	For example, *engine*, *matter*, *treaty*, or *pact*.
Roots	Meaningful units that can be joined together to form words. Roots cannot stand alone as words; they need to be joined with other morphemes to create words.	For example, the word *interject* contains the morphemes *inter-* and *-ject*.
Prefixes	A group of letters (morpheme) added before a word or root to alter its meaning.	For example, in the words *retract*, *reevaluate*, and *reexamine* the prefix *re-*appears in the words.
Suffixes	A group of letters (morpheme) added after a word or root. Suffixes can include derivational and inflectional morphemes.	For example, in the words *addition*, *classification*, and *declaration* the suffix *-tion* appears in the words.
Derivational Suffix	A suffix added to the end of a word that can change the grammatical category of the word.	For example, *teach* (v), *teacher* (n). Adding *–er* changes the word from a verb to a noun in this case.
Inflectional Suffix	A suffix added to the end of a word that can change the grammatical properties of a word. It does not change the meaning of the word but impacts the grammatical class.	For example, a suffix determines verb tense, gender, and degree. Adding *-ing* to a word signals present tense. Adding *-es* to a word signals the noun is plural.

Teaching morphology helps students become strategic in reading words, spelling words, and comprehending text. It supports students in making sense of unfamiliar words by analyzing words by their individual parts. For example, the words *teacher* and *driver* contain two morphemes, a base word, and a suffix. The suffix common in both words is *-er*. This suffix means "one who takes part in," therefore *teacher* means someone who takes part in the act of teaching and a *driver* is someone who drives. We can further break down the meaning of the words by analyzing the base words, *teach* and *drive*.

Knowledge of morphemes helps students strategically understand words by their meaning. They can make sense of many unfamiliar words that contain morphemes with which they are familiar. Students need to engage in the deconstruction of language, breaking language down in to its smallest parts to strategically decipher meaning.

Written Discourse

Too often, writing instruction is incidental, and students are simply asked to write but not taught how to write. They are given directions to create brainstorming webs and to convert their webs to a draft. They are provided feedback on the draft, correct their papers, recopy, and repeat until it is acceptable for the teacher. The problem with this process is that students do not always see the corrections they are making. They do not understand why the teacher marked up their papers; they simply recopy and follow the teacher's directions. In addition, many students are not always aware of what a draft looks like, depending on the genre in which they are writing.

I have spent nearly ten years training teachers on teaching writing. In my experience, I found that first and foremost I needed to develop the teachers' confidence as teachers of writing. I needed them to experience what it means to write across genres and improve their own writing. For many teachers, it was a new experience. When I would ask teachers to identify a writing genre for a unit of study, they did not hesitate. They would immediately think about the kind of reading involved in the unit and connect it directly to the writing they would require of students. For example, if a language arts unit required students to read fantasy stories, the teachers would ask students to write a fantasy story. Though teachers would quickly identify what to write, when I asked the teachers to write a sample themselves, they often froze. They started asking themselves, "What does a fantasy story include again?" "How does a fantasy story start?" "What makes a fantasy a fantasy?" They would then ask me, "Can we have some time to go to the library and find some fantasy stories?" "Can we get our teacher's guide and read over the fantasy stories?"

I always enjoyed this activity because it was a harsh reality for teachers in that we ourselves require students to be successful writers and yet we do not provide our students with the same support. For example, the teachers began their writing by seeking resources that would help support them as writers. They kept a running list of materials they used. Once that was done, together they brainstormed the characteristics that make up the fantasy genre. Upon completing that, they were ready to begin writing. As they wrote, they often stopped to ask their colleagues to check their work and asked the same from me. This led to an understanding of a process, one where they can support their students as writers:

1. Explore the genre or writing task.

2. Share resources, such as samples of text written in the selected genre.

3. Take note of similarities across the resources. This will help you identify the elements of the genre.

4. Begin to draft some ideas.

5. Provide opportunities for peer feedback along the way.

6. Have resources available throughout the process.

With students, it is important to provide explicit instruction in written discourse and structure. This is best done through modeling appropriate written discourse and providing mini-lessons on grammar, written structure, flow of ideas, and elements of the genre. I have found workshop models to be most successful when working with English language learners.

Stemming from the work of Lucy Calkins (1994) and the reading and writing project, I have developed and used a workshop model that has been successful with English language learners (see table below and on the following page). What differs from my model and Calkins' model is the intentional opportunities for oral rehearsal and oral peer interaction. Calkins does mention the importance of these elements; however, I have made them a part of every workshop session.

Writer's Workshop for English Language Learners

Mini-lesson **(10–15 minutes)**	In a whole-group setting, the teacher explicitly models writing expectations. This includes directed lessons on a writing skill or strategy, grammar instruction for editing, analyzing samples of writing, reading text that teaches a writing skill or strategy, and demonstrating how to engage in peer reviewing.
Oral Rehearsal/ Informal Assessment and Support **(2–3 minutes)**	When applicable, after a mini-lesson, allow students time to orally share with partners what they plan to do that day as writers. This includes talking about the mini-lesson and thinking through their own writing and ideas. This gives English language learners a chance to check for understanding with a peer about the mini-lesson and to rehearse their ideas for writing. While students are talking, this is an opportunity for teachers to informally listen to what students are saying. The teacher can assess their initial understanding of the mini-lesson and listen to the language they are bringing to the writing experience. This helps teachers prepare for future mini-lessons.

Independent Writing/Teacher Conferring **(20–40 minutes)**	As students work independently, the teacher formally meets with students to discuss their writing and their processes as writers. This is a chance for teachers to differentiate instruction. The teacher is meeting one-on-one with a student and providing instruction or support on his or her individual needs. I highly encourage teachers to meet with their students at the students' desk. By asking students to come to the teacher's desk, it interrupts their writing and takes them out of their comfortable writing space. If there is a group of students with a similar writing need, this is a good time to work with a small guided-writing group. The amount of time given for independent writing varies by grade level. For kindergarten students, 20 minutes is a good start, increasing 10 minutes each year per grade level.
Peer Share/ Informal Assessment and Support **(2–3 minutes)**	After independent writing, English language learners should be able to try out their written language with a peer. They can read to their peers what they wrote that day. In return they receive immediate feedback. This provides the teacher with another opportunity to informally assess what the students are sharing orally about their writing.
Community Circle **(2–3 minutes)**	Gathering the class together as a whole group after a writing session is important for building community. This is a chance for students to share their processes, strategies, progress, or the ideas they incorporated. Giving students the opportunity to share their experiences will make them feel successful.

For English language learners, I further encourage teachers to provide explicit instruction on written discourse during mini-lessons early on in the writing process.

Scaffolding Writing

English language learners can produce amazing writing samples in English when provided with explicit writing instruction. Many teachers I have worked with have shared that they wait to teach writing until their English language learners have reached a basic proficiency level in English. I would argue that with the right support, they could be amazing writers even at early levels of second-language acquisition. A kindergarten English language learner wrote the writing sample in figure 5.4 below after only three months in school. You can see the student's knowledge of phonics and story. Figure 5.5 on page 108 demonstrates a kindergarten student using detailed drawings as a source of storytelling. He has the ideas and the knowledge of narratives. He is still working on developing the English words necessary to tell his story in print.

Fig. 5.4 Writing Sample of a Kindergartner

Fig. 5.5 A Kindergartner's Example of Using Detailed Drawings

In addition, figures 5.6 and 5.7 on page 109 demonstrate writing samples of fourth-grade English language learners at an intermediate level of second-language acquisition. You can see how well they are able to write if we believe in them and give them the structured opportunities to do so. There is a free flow of ideas in their writing, demonstrating a clear connection between their English fluency and writing.

Fig. 5.6 Example of an Excerpt From a Fourth Grader

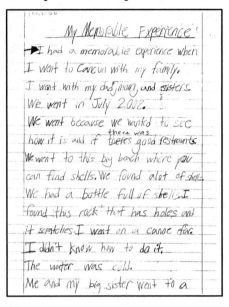

Fig. 5.7 Another Example of an Excerpt From a Fourth Grader

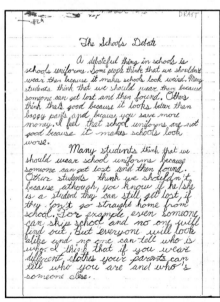

The support that English language learners often need when writing includes explicit instruction in written discourse. This includes understanding the elements of a genre, the structure, and the organization of the piece of writing. It includes understanding how the ideas are put together to meet a given purpose and communicate effectively. My recommendation to teachers of English language learners is that they scaffold the draft stage of the writing process. Typically, we spend a great deal of time in the pre-writing stage, preparing students to write within a given genre. However, we do not always explicitly show them how to take those ideas and craft them into a written piece. Scaffolding the draft means writing in chunks.

Classroom Connection

To prepare her fifth-grade students for persuasive writing, Mrs. Vasquez began by reading the story *Earrings!* by Judith Viorst. She stopped frequently, asking the class to share their specific arguments and responses to the plot. After reading the story, Mrs. Vasquez created a chart titled *Elements of Persuasive Writing*. On her chart, she included the words *argument*, *counterargument*, *response*, and *position*. Using the text as an example, the students identified how the young girl in the story persuaded her parents to let her get her ears pierced. This ended the writing lesson for the day. The following day, Mrs. Vasquez told the students that they would be writing their own persuasive essays. They were able to pick their own topics and they completed graphic organizers that captured all the elements of persuasive writing. The next day, students began to draft only the introduction of the essay. Mrs. Vasquez showed the class sample essays and asked them what they noticed about the introductions. "What information belongs in the introduction?" The students shared that there was a catchy opening, a strong thesis statement, and an introduction to the topics of the upcoming paragraphs, which included arguments and counterarguments. The students were then directed to begin drafting their introductions. Figure 5.8 below provides a sample of a student's progress in writing her persuasive essay in Mrs. Vasquez's class.

From this point on, Mrs. Vasquez provided explicit mini-lessons on grammar and fluency to strengthen the students' introductory paragraphs before moving on to the body of the essay. Teachers should be just as intentional and explicit throughout each part of the essay, breaking it down one section at a time. This helps English language learners focus on smaller units of writing. When the genre is revisited later in the year, teachers can begin to pull back on the scaffolds as students develop as writers.

Fig. 5.8 Sample of a Student's Progress in Writing a Persuasive Essay

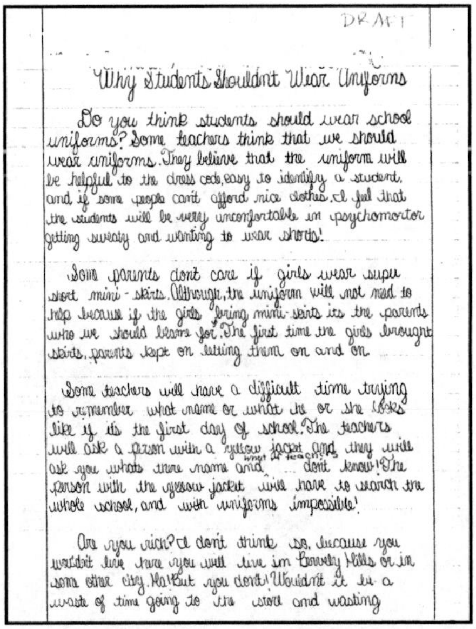
DRAFT

Why Students Shouldnt Wear Uniforms

Do you think students should wear school uniforms? Some teachers think that we should wear uniforms. They believe that the uniform will be helpful to the dress code, easy to identify a student, and if some people cant afford nice clothes. I feel that the students will be very unconfortable in psychomortor getting sweaty and wanting to wear shorts!

Some parents dont care if girls wear super short mini-skirts. Although, the uniform will not need to help because if the girls bring mini-skirts its the parents who we should blame for. The first time the girls brought skirts, parents kept on letting them on and on.

Some teachers will have a difficult time trying to remember what name or what he or she looks like if its the first day of school. The teachers will ask a person with a yellow jacket and they will ask you whats there name and what it teachers dont know! The person with the yellow jacket will have to search the whole school, and with uniforms impossible!

Are you rich? I dont think so, because you wouldnt live here you will live in Beverly Hills or in some other city. Ha! But you dont! Wouldnt it be a waste of time going to the store and wasting

Reading and Writing Connections

In a fourth-grade class I visited often, students were engaged in a unit called "Mystery to Medicine." They were exposed to a lot of expository text that not only showed the written genre of exposition, but also provided students with the content knowledge needed to write exposition. The teacher created a useful chart with students that showed students how the work they were doing as readers could support their work as writers. The teacher had explored the stories from the perspective of a writer, pulling out key elements and good uses of written language as models. This reading and writing connection is critical for students to understand as they become independent writers. They will need to understand how to be learners of writing beyond school. Figure 5.9 below is a chart that was created by a third-grade teacher with her students. As they read stories, they chart the elements of the story and use it as a tool for writing narratives.

Fig. 5.9 Elements Scholars Use in Their Writing

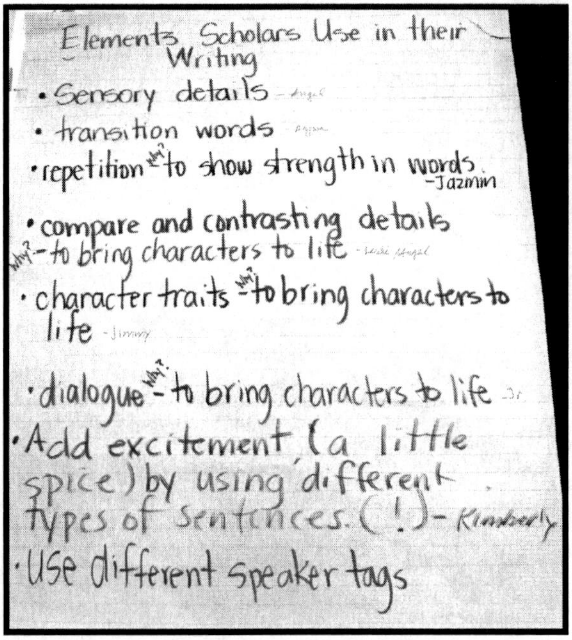

Authentic Writing Opportunities

I am a strong believer in making a student's learning relevant and meaningful. In writing instruction, this can be accomplished by allowing students to see authentic reasons for writing. Where in real life will they see expository, narrative, and persuasive writing? For example, if students are engaged in a persuasive-writing unit, they can work through their essays carefully to develop English written discourse. But when it comes time to publish, students can create a commercial script about their essays. What were they fighting for or what were they trying to convince others of? This authentic form of writing shows student writing is something they will encounter in the real world. It is not solely for school but for communicating their thinking in written form, in and beyond school.

Strategies for Teaching Reading Comprehension

Reading-comprehension strategies support students when they encounter unfamiliar text. We teach students how to make meaning from difficult text, initially at a recall level, leading to a level of critical and creative thinking. "The purpose of specifically teaching critical thinking…is to improve the thinking skills of students and thus better prepare them to succeed in the world" (Shafersman 1991). Students are exposed to information all day, every day. Information is presented from multiple perspectives and through a variety of sources. Accessing information is not the problem today. It is literally at their fingertips. Through cell phones and the Internet, you can look up anything in a moment's time. The challenge, however, is to teach students to know what to do with the information to which they have access. They need to become critical consumers of the information they find. They need to question the information, and analyze its source and credibility. They need to distinguish between good information and bad information. We want students to challenge their thinking and to be able to justify their ideas through valid, credible sources of information.

To help students reach this level of comprehension and

literacy development, we begin by helping them access sources of information, draw meaning when reading, and learn to read deeply within and across additional sources of information. Some strategies I have found successful when helping English language learners make meaning from text include Sticky Notes, Reflective Journals, Inquiry Charts, and SQPRRR/SQP3R.

Sticky Notes

Sticky Notes are a tool that can help support students' reading comprehension. I like to think about Sticky Notes as "thinking markers." Most students in public schools are not allowed to write in their textbooks. As a reader myself, I love to write all over my books. When I am reading to learn, I mark up the text, write in the margins, highlight, and earmark favorite pages. Yet we sometimes deny students these critical-thinking strategies. Using Sticky Notes allows students the opportunity to mark up their texts and make a note of their thinking. They can tag favorite parts, write comments, write key vocabulary or learning points, and write questions about challenging parts to refer back to. The key is to show students how to use the Sticky Notes and make them an explicit part of your instruction. This means demonstrating through think-alouds where and for what purpose you would use a Sticky Note. Demonstrate how to come back to the Sticky Notes and why. Sticky Notes are especially useful when students are asked to justify their thinking. It takes them right back to the location in the text. This strategy gives English language learners a tool for tracking their thinking and learning and allowing them to talk with peers or their teacher when language interferes with thinking.

Sticky Notes can be helpful within the different content areas. For example, in mathematics if students are working on a word problem, they can make notes on their Sticky Notes of the parts of the problem that are confusing. They can further take notes on the information or cue words within the problem that can help them decide what the problem is asking them to do. This strategy is similar to what students would do if they could write in their textbooks. They can underline key words such as *in all* and *together*.

Without the ability to write in their books, the sticky notes once again provide a great resource for students to document their thoughts and questions.

Reflective Journals

Similar to Sticky Notes, I encourage teachers to use Reflective Journals with English language learners. Reflective Journals serve as a place for students to record their thinking. Again, this strategy helps English language learners jot down what was confusing or what language interfered with their comprehension of the text. It is a great way to develop written fluency, because students do not need to worry about conventions and written discourse. It is a place where students engage in a free flow of ideas. They reflect on what they have learned and do not worry about perfection. It is a personal Reflective Journal that also serves as a resource for students. They can refer back to their journals to see what they have learned as they begin a new lesson. I recommend that teachers use a Reflective Journal across the curriculum. Whether the teacher calls it a notebook, a journal, or a learning log—what is important is that students have a place to reflect and document their thinking regularly. When I taught first grade, my students used to keep a math journal that would serve as a record of their metacognitive thinking when solving a math problem. For example, after they completed a word problem they would write, "I started by drawing two circles for the balls and then I drew four lines for the bats and then I counted them all together and I got six." It was a record of their thinking and the process they used to solve their math problems. My students also kept science journals, literacy response journals, and an art journal. Having Reflective Journals provides teachers with the opportunity to monitor students' learning across the curriculum.

Inquiry Charts

Graphic organizers and tables are helpful for English language learners in organizing their thinking. There are a large variety of graphic organizers that can help students think about their learning in different ways. This format is nonthreatening because English language learners can record their thinking in shorter bits of language and challenge their thinking. A type of chart I especially like for all students is an Inquiry Chart. An Inquiry Chart is a kind of T-chart that takes students from basic recall of information to questioning their thinking and learning. As students observe or read something, they can jot down what they learned or understood on one side and then generate questions on the other. This is helpful in guiding students' learning as they explore the topic further. Inquiry Charts can be used across the curriculum. They also provide teachers with a form of assessment whereby students are sharing what they understand and what they have yet to understand about the content at hand.

Survey, Question, Predict, Read, Recite, Review (SQPRRR/SQP3R)

In his discussion of the strategy *survey, question, predict, read, recite,* and *review,* Francis Robinson (1960) explained about the importance of students preparing for a focused reading experience. Students generate prior knowledge and focus their reading with opportunities to revisit their thinking for deeper comprehension. SQPRRR/SQP3R is most effective when used with expository text. These texts provide headings and subheadings, allowing students to organize their thinking as readers and use the strategy successfully. Teachers should model for students every step of the process before asking students to engage in it on their own. Though I have seen premade tables of SQPRRR/SQP3R, I recommend completing the strategy in a notebook. The pre-made tables can limit the space for students to write their thinking and learning. Students will need to follow the labels in their notebooks as they move through the strategy (see the table on page 118). This gives students all the space needed to complete every step of the process. Figure 5.10 on page 117 provides an example of an SQPRRR/SQP3R entries in a student's science notebook during a unit of study on environments. In this example, the student had read the first part of the chapter on deserts.

Survey, Question, Predict, Read, Recite, Review

Survey	The teacher identifies how much of the text students will read. It is a good idea to chunk the text for SQPRRR/SQP3R, ideally no more than a couple of subheadings at a time. Once the teacher identifies what will be read, the text is *surveyed*. This means browsing through it, noting anything that stands out (e.g., words, information, images, charts, diagrams). Students independently jot down some notes. They are also reminded that they should be browsing, not reading.
Question	All of the headings and subheadings are located and turned into *questions*. For example, if the heading reads *Animals of the Rainforest*, the teacher can can model writing a question, "Which animals live in the rainforest?"
Predict	For each question the class writes, students use the survey notes and their prior knowledge to *predict* the answers to the questions. Again, students are reminded not to read. They are still in the pre-reading phase of preparing to read, focusing their reading and generating prior knowledge.
Read	Now it is time to *read*. At this point the teacher decides if he or she wants students to read the selection on their own, in class, or for homework. The teacher can also read it to them as a read-aloud or even have them read it with partners. As students are reading, they are encouraged to take notes on the information they read that addresses their questions.
Recite	Students *recite* with peers what they have learned up to this point based on all of the notes taken during the survey, question, predict, and read portions of the process. This is a critical step for English language learners. They get to check for understanding with a peer and rehearse academic language.
Review	With partners or in small groups, students create a review guide based on the discussion of the text (during recite). This is similar to a summary sheet, where they note the main ideas, key vocabulary, big ideas, or concepts. This review is a great resource for students as they continue to read. It can also serve as a study guide for the future.

Fig. 5.10 Example of a Science Notebook Integrating SQPRRR/SQP3R

Student Investment

The remaining key elements of a holistic literacy program for English language learners have a common theme I call student investment. Generating prior knowledge, tapping into motivation, and building reading fluency all empower students to be active participants in their learning.

When generating prior knowledge, we facilitate comprehension. Research in cognitive psychology has shown that people learn best when they can build upon prior experiences and knowledge. For this reason, I encourage teachers to begin their units of study with a warm-up that provides students some background knowledge. This can include showing a short video or a slide show of images related to the unit, or reading aloud to students from multiple sources of information. Students will see that they know a lot more then they initially thought when they are exposed to these meaningful images, videos, and texts. At best, we provide the actual experience; but when this is not possible, videos, pictures, and text offers great exposure, as well.

Using literature that is relevant and meaningful to students further supports activating prior knowledge. The more we can do to connect learning to students' experiences, the more prior knowledge they will bring to their learning. This facilitates comprehension and motivates students because they are learning something familiar and nonthreatening.

Motivation

Motivating students to want to read is a challenge, but it can lead to high levels of literacy and language development. As a child, I can remember reading being a task only for school. We did not have many books in our home, and my class texts included the *Dick and Jane* book series and anthologies. I was not exposed to reading for pleasure. I thought the purpose of reading was to do well in school. As an adult, I have seen the benefits and joy of reading. I think about all of the things I missed as a child by not reading for pleasure. I find myself buying books all of the time. I want my students and my own children to see books in a way I did not. I want to promote reading for pleasure.

Students need to be surrounded by books of a variety of genres, topics, types, and styles. When I taught first grade, I had a student who did not enjoy reading. One day, his mother shared with me that dinosaurs fascinated him. That evening, I rushed to the bookstore and bought all the books I could find about dinosaurs. The following day, I could not get him to stop reading! Students need to make connections to books. They need opportunities in school to explore books and have time to read independently. This gives them a chance to see how much books have to offer. Indirectly, the more students read, the better their vocabulary, reading comprehension, and ultimately success in school will be (Stanovich 1986). Avid readers are exposed to a lot of language in context. They see how words are used and what they mean. This contextualized exposure to language can facilitate second-language acquisition (Krashen 2004).

The best way to build reading fluency is to give students frequent opportunities to read books at their individual reading level. We cannot build reading fluency by forcing students to struggle through texts that are beyond their literacy and language development levels. If they cannot make meaning of what they read, they will become frustrated. Then, students will not want to read because they feel unsuccessful and do not see a purpose in sounding out words that do not make sense. Students need access to books at their reading levels to build fluency. This, coupled with explicit instruction in phonics, phonemic awareness, comprehension, vocabulary, and morphology, will help students reach higher levels of literacy.

Conclusion

The concept of developing literacy is multifaceted. Teachers provide students with the necessary tools to make sense of text. This includes knowledge of phonemic awareness, phonics, vocabulary, morphology, comprehension reading skills, and strategies in writing instruction. Together, these tools help students strategically comprehend text and create original pieces of writing. In addition, we must be mindful of what it means for English language learners to learn to read in a second language. The table below provides a summary of the essential elements discussed throughout this chapter when facilitating second-language literacy for English language learners.

Essential Elements in Facilitating Second-Language Literacy

Learning to read in a primary language supports:
- frequent and varied opportunities for developing oral language
- building explicit phonemic awareness and phonics instruction through integrating diverse instructional methods
- explicit vocabulary instruction with opportunities to use words in and out of context and across the curriculum
- explicit teaching of written discourse
- opportunities to see and create authentic forms of writing
- explicit teaching or reading comprehension strategies
- building prior knowledge
- providing students access to a variety of texts
- providing opportunities for independent reading

Reflection Questions

1. What opportunities do you provide for your students to become critical and creative thinkers?

2. What kind of support can you provide your students to scaffold written discourse?

3. How have you encouraged a love of reading in your students? What has worked best?

4. What do you know about your students and their personal experiences?

5. How can you fill in the gaps when generating prior knowledge?

6. How can you teach phonemic awareness and phonics through different approaches to ensure that all students develop strong foundational skills?

Developing Language Across the Curriculum

"Language should be an ever-developing procedure and not an isolated occurrence."

— Robert Smithson

English language development is part of a student's entire day as he or she tries to make sense of spoken language, written language, complex content vocabulary, and concrete and abstract concepts. Successful programs for English language learners provide focused time for ELD as well as purposeful, explicit language instruction throughout the day and academic-content instruction (Goldenberg 2008). **In my work with teachers involved in ELD, Content ELD, and Academic Language Development (ALD) I have discovered that there is a lot of confusion around the definition and purpose of each term.** Developing a common understanding of these terms helps teachers understand what it means to support English language learners throughout the day. Let us start by defining ELD, followed by an explanation of Content ELD and ALD.

English Language Development

ELD and ESL instruction have often been used synonymously. Depending on where you teach and the level you teach, states and districts may use one term over another. "The purpose of ESL/ELD is to enable English language learners to master the skills of listening, speaking, reading, and writing in English to the extent that they are able to use the English language appropriately and effectively for authentic communicative purposes and achieve academic success in English-language mainstream classrooms" (Wright 2010, 82). Typically, states and districts require teachers to provide a set time of day specifically for ELD. In my work as a professional developer, I have found this time of day to vary from 35 minutes in a kindergarten classroom to an hour of ELD in first- through fifth-grade settings. I have worked in school districts where ELD instruction is provided by the classroom teacher to a mixed group of English language learners. A mixed group is a class of English language learners at different levels of second-language development. This model is favored by some districts to provide English language learners with different language models to support second language acquisition. I have also worked with districts that reorganize students during ELD time, where they cluster students based on their ELD level. The benefits of clustering English language learners during ELD is that teachers can target language instruction specifically to the needs of students at common levels of ELD. Having taught, observed, and researched both models, I have found the latter (clustering students during ELD) to be most effective, *but only* when English language learners are mixed throughout the rest of their instructional day. Having peers as language models when engaging in discussions is important to support ongoing language development.

Claude Goldenberg (2008, 42) in his article, "Teaching English Language Learners: What the research does—and does not—say" explains,

> ELLs need intensive oral English language development (ELD), especially vocabulary and academic English instruction...we have much to learn about what type of ELD instruction is most beneficial. Effective ELD provides both explicit teaching of features of English (such as syntax, grammar, vocabulary, pronunciation, and norms of social usage) and ample, meaningful opportunities to use English—but we do not know whether there is an optimal balance between the two (much less what it might be).

What happens during ELD varies greatly. But what we do know is that students must receive explicit instruction in academic *vocabulary, functions and forms,* and opportunities to develop oral and written *fluency.* These concepts are explained in greater detail in chapters 3 and 5.

Vocabulary, functions and forms, and fluency include part of "what" we foster in English language learners during ELD, though there are many other components to ELD. Part of the work of language forms is understanding the structure of the forms, the grammatical composition, and how to construct language for a variety of purposes. Grammar is a large part of ELD, as is reading comprehension and writing development. In my work in ELD, we have heavily focused on the vocabulary, and the functions and forms of language from comprehension to usage mainly because they have been missing for years in ELD/ESL instruction. Grammar, reading, and writing have traditionally been the focus of many ELD/ESL programs. Focusing on vocabulary, functions and forms, and fluency empower English language learners to develop oral and written fluency and to truly develop academic language for academic and life-long success. It takes traditional instruction to the level of application.

Thinking further about ELD and how to support English language learners, Drs. Dolores Beltran and Lilia Sarmiento (2010) developed a framework for ELD based on three overlapping and interacting dimensions: talk, thought, and interaction. This framework guides teachers as they think about "how" to implement lessons that can effectively develop academic English. Together, Dr. Beltran, Dr. Sarmiento, and I have collectively provided over ten years of professional development on ELD. As part of ongoing professional development, research, and practice, we have refined and strengthened our beliefs about how best to facilitate ELD. What we have found to remain true as we continue to improve our practices pertaining to ELD is that every lesson designed to support English language learners must include *talk*, *thought*, and *interaction* (see table below).

Talk, Thought, and Interaction

Talk	Students need opportunities to engage in oral discourse. They need to hear language models and use language themselves to develop oral fluency. Providing students with engaging activities across the curriculum where they can share their thinking and learning with one another exposes them to academic language. They hear what it sounds like to use language for a variety of purposes and hear vocabulary used in context.
Thought	The connection between language and thought is evident when students are provided opportunities to develop high levels of cognition, engage in critical thinking, and share their thinking with one another. The thinking we require of students leads to the talk that they will use to share their thinking.
Interaction	The dialogic and mediated exchanges between users of a language create authentic opportunities to acquire language. Social interaction plays an important role in second-language acquisition, including exchanges between teacher and student and between students.

Facilitating thought, talk, and interaction takes a great deal of planning and decision making. We need to understand second-language acquisition, know where our students are in their language development, and know how to scaffold instruction accordingly. We need to select the appropriate strategies to meet our objectives and our students' needs. This has long been the challenge teachers face when using standardized, scripted curricula. Teachers feel trapped, lock-stepped within the program, and are afraid to step outside the program or to modify the program to support their students. I can remember feeling this way until I began to reflect on my teaching and my students' learning. What kind of students was I developing? Were my students meeting their potential? Have I provided a curriculum that is demanding, and yet tailored to individual needs? Were my students, in fact, learning? These questions led me to reconsider my perspective and use of curricular programs.

I have found all curricular programs to be good resources in my instructional planning. They are a source of information, ideas, and strategies that I can use with my students. The challenge is to make sure that the lessons are meeting the needs of *your* students. This is what is so empowering about *talk, thought,* and *interaction*. When working with English language learners, every lesson we create—or re-create—must have opportunities for talk, thought, and interaction. We need to scaffold our talk and provide opportunities for students to engage in thoughtful discussions with different peers about challenging content. Talk alone is not enough; it must be grounded in concepts, ideas, and content. Thought must be challenged as students develop critical and creative thinking skills. And interaction must be complex; from working with different peers to exploring a variety of materials.

Strategies for Teaching ELD

Some strategies I have found to be successful during ELD include Tea Party, Travelers and Talkers, Lines of Communication, World in a Bag, and Four-Corner Literature Review. Many of the wonderful strategies I have learned come from the work of

Project GLAD (Guided Language Acquisition Design) or have been created or modified through my work with teachers as a professional developer. I have found that all of these strategies can be used within any curricular program.

Tea Party

The purpose of Tea Party is for students to share their thinking with their classmates. It provides an opportunity for English language learners to develop oral fluency because they have a chance to orally rehearse their thinking with multiple partners. A Tea Party begins with the teacher deciding what it is that students will talk about when they engage in the Tea Party. I have seen teachers provide students with quotes, a topic, a picture, a sheet of paper with text, a math problem, or a tangible item. The teacher then models for students how to walk around and talk with their classmates. For example, if students are provided a quote, the teacher would model reading the quote first, and then say, "I think it means…" Students are then given a quote and asked to stand up. They are directed to move around the room, stopping to talk with classmates about their quotes. They share their quote and their thoughts and then move on to another partner. After a few minutes, the teacher asks students to return to their seats. During a Tea Party, the teacher walks around monitoring partnerships, making sure students are moving on and talking to different classmates, informally assessing language, and ensuring that everyone has a partner.

Tea Party can be used with students at all levels of second-language acquisition. Some modifications you might make for beginners include the following:

- Provide students with sentence frames to use as they walk around and talk to a peer.

- Partner students if they are in the earliest (silent) stage of second-language acquisition. This helps them implement language and more importantly hear models of language in context.

When working with middle-school students, I found that they prefer to call it "the social" or "the mixer." As silly as it may sound, a group of sixth graders told me that "Tea Party" sounded too "cutesy" and "for little kids." In any case, whatever you decide to call it, Tea Party supports students' ELD because students are able to share their thinking orally—allowing for fluency to develop as they repeat their thoughts from one partner to the next.

In addition, the teacher can guide the talk by focusing on a particular language function. For example, if the class has been working on the function of compare and contrast, the teacher might provide students with a picture and tell the class that when they work with partners, they are to compare and contrast their pictures. For English language learners, the teacher can provide appropriate sentence frames for students' second-language acquisition level.

Travelers and Talkers

The purpose of this strategy is for students to share their thinking and learning visually and orally. Based on the content learned, the teacher selects key vocabulary or concepts from the unit. For example, when I taught the American Revolution, I used the terms *conflict, emancipation, secession, abolition, opposition, rebel,* and *fugitive.* These were high-frequency content words we had studied and applied to the Civil War.

To implement Travelers and Talkers, students are placed into groups of four and provided with a poster size sheet of paper and a sheet of 8½" x 11" white paper. Each group is assigned a term/concept. Students are given two-three minutes to discuss the term/concept. As a group, they then decide on a visual representation of the term or concept (five minutes). There should not be any words on the page; the goal is to visually represent the meaning of the term/concept. Students take 10 minutes to draw the visual on the large poster paper and a replica on the small sheet of paper (students should draw both visuals at the same time). When students finish their visual, they take two-three minutes to discuss the visual and make sure that all group members can explain the meaning of the term or concept as represented through the visual. After their discussions, the large visual is hung somewhere around the room. The group is responsible for selecting two "travelers" and two "talkers." (If there is an odd-numbered group, there should be at least two travelers and the other members can be the talkers.) Students who are assigned as the "talkers" find their posters around the room and stand next to them. These students are to remain at their group poster for the entire sharing time. Students who are assigned as the "travelers" are responsible for taking the small group-created replica of the visual and standing near their group poster. They are also the ones traveling and moving from poster to poster when signaled. As students move from poster to poster, the "talkers" share for a few minutes the term or concept they selected and the visual representation they made with students who are the "travelers."

On average, this activity takes about 35–45 minutes depending on how many groups there are. Of all the strategies I have implemented with students and have observed, this has been a favorite among teachers and students. It adds a great deal to students' vocabulary, functions, forms, and fluency development.

To extend this activity, ask students to each create a visual representation of their thinking. This is a real challenge, because most of the terms/concepts selected are typically abstract concepts. This extension demonstrates a high level of comprehension of the term/concept. All students will only hear and see the meaning of the terms through their peers' visuals. Through this activity, students are typically practicing the functions of explaining or defining. Again, if the teacher feels it is necessary, her or she can provide sentence frames for students to practice, as they talk about their term/concept. I have even seen teachers ask students to carry around a "passport" and take notes as they travel from one poster to the next. Figures 6.1 and 6.2 on page 131 are examples of students engaging in this activity and what it means to create a visual representation.

Fig. 6.1 Visual Representation for Travelers and Talkers

Fig. 6.2 Students Engaging in Travelers and Talkers

Lines of Communication

The purpose of this strategy is for students to gather information, share their learning, and record their classmates' thinking and learning. This is a complex strategy, but beneficial for developing the functions of asking questions, clarifying, and explaining. I recommend using this strategy as a pre-reading, pre-unit activity. It helps generate prior knowledge and allows the teacher to hear what students are bringing to the learning experience. Teachers can also use it as an end-of-unit strategy in which students will share what they have learned.

Lines of Communication begins with questions. The teacher provides questions or asks students to generate questions based on a theme or unit of study. For example, when studying about the environment, students brainstormed the following questions:

1. What is global warming?

2. How can we help take care of Earth?

3. What is recycling and how can we help?

4. What is pollution and how can we help?

5. What happens when we litter?

I had shared with students that we were going to be talking about our environment and how we are connected to the world around us. I then showed students a series of slides and asked them to generate questions based on what they saw. (The teacher can also provide questions to students.) Once the questions are generated, the classroom is arranged into pods of 10, with five chairs on each side facing one another. Students then take a notebook and a writing utensil to a vacant chair and are numbered by five and informed that their number coincides with the number of question(s) for which they will be responsible to answer. At this point, students are already sitting at a pod so they are face-to-face with a classmate. I encourage students to be knee-to-knee so they are close enough to hear when the activity begins. The teacher designates one side as Group A, and the other as Group B. When the activity begins, students sitting on the side designated as Group A ask the student sitting in front of them the question they wrote in their notebooks. The partner who asked the question will then take notes on what his or her partner is sharing. Once they have responded, the partner on the Group B side will ask their question and take notes. After a few minutes, the teacher signals for students to stop. The teacher tells students in Group B to stand up and students in Group A to remain seated. Group B shifts one chair to its right. Once they sit down the teacher signals the conversations to begin again and Group A asks their new partner their question, and Group B once again responds. Group B then asks their question and Group A responds. Again students should be taking notes in their notebook of what their partners are saying. The procedure continues until Group B moves through the line. When students are asked their same question, inform them that it is their opportunity to share their thoughts about that particular question. When students are finished asking questions, the teacher asks students to regroup based on the number of their question(s). So, students who asked the same questions are in the same group. Students then discuss with their peers their question(s) and what was shared about their question.

Lines of Communication is beneficial for generating background knowledge that students may not have possessed before. Hearing the knowledge their classmates bring to the table helps begin the learning process. They have more schema from which to build. It also provides a great opportunity for an informal assessment of students' content knowledge as they begin a unit of study. This helps the teacher decide where to begin and what to build on. If you are using Lines of Communication as an end-of-unit activity, it can be an informal assessment demonstrating what your students learned and understood about the unit or content. Remembering that ELD also includes reading, Lines of Communication is a strategy that helps fill the gap for students who have limited background knowledge.

World in a Bag

The purpose of World in a Bag is to develop students' observation and inquiry-based skills and to rehearse predetermined language functions and forms. Based on the unit of study, the teacher would gather items that represent the lesson at hand. For example, a third-grade unit on rocks can include lots of different rocks for students to explore. I personally like to use the large sealable bags for this activity, making it easy to store and distribute materials. I recommend about 6–8 items per bag. Once the items are collected, the teacher thinks about the language objective(s) for the unit to create questions for exploring the items. For example, if we are studying rocks and working on the language functions of describing and comparing, I would guide students to talk and write about the rocks in the bag, using identifying and comparing forms of language.

To begin this activity, students are placed into groups of four and provided with a bag of items representing the lesson. Students are then given the opportunity to explore and examine the items. After a few minutes, each student selects one of the items and he or she writes down any observations and questions that he or she has about the item. Once they are finished writing, students share their item and writing with their group. This allows students to hear different forms of language from their peers description and questioning. After about five minutes, the teacher guides students through a structured language activity. Students are given the following three questions to respond to in their notebooks:

1. Write three words that describe your object.

2. Describe your object using complete sentences.

3. Write two sentences that compare your object to those of your partners.

When students are finished answering the questions, they share their writing with a partner in their group. As students are sharing, the teacher walks around and observes the forms of language that students are using to describe and compare, as well as the language functions and forms used during the activity. Teachers should record the language forms used on chart paper. This informs students of the language they are already using and helps teachers in creating goals for advanced forms of language to explicitly teach and share with students.

Keep in mind that the language functions and forms you generate should be selected based on the language objective. Therefore, the questions mentioned as examples on page 134 were particular to the example of rocks and the functions of description and comparison. These will change as will the items in the bag based on your content and language objectives.

Four-Corner Literature Review

The purpose of Four-Corner Literature Review is for students to read varied sources of information to support content or concept development. This is a great activity for supporting struggling readers and making content accessible to all. It involves providing students with different forms of text addressing the same concept or topic. The teacher searches for four different sources of text for the selected area of study. A lot of different sources can be found online or from different textbooks or trade books. The texts should differ in structure and readability. Once the four text samples have been selected, the teacher makes sure there are at least 8–10 copies of each selected text. The text is introduced to the class and students are informed that they will each select one that they want to read and report on. After the teacher has shared a little about each text, the text is distributed in the four corners of the classroom. Students then stand in the corner of the text they have selected. Once everyone has selected a corner, students take a copy of the text and return to their seats. Students then each read their texts and highlight any important parts. After a few minutes, students are directed to find their classmates who read the same text and discuss what they just read. If there is a text that was read by only one student, the teacher incorporates the students into another group to share what was read. Ideally, all texts will have at least two readers so that discussions help clarify information and support the meaning-making process. After the groups talk about their texts, each group shares two key points with the class. Students' ideas are recorded on chart paper for future reference.

What I like about Four-Corner Literature Review is that all students feel successful as readers. They all select a text with which they feel comfortable, and they are given an opportunity to talk with others who have read the same text to clarify any uncertainties. In addition, it allows students to introduce varied sources of information and extend their learning beyond the textbook. I have found this strategy very helpful in supporting English language learners, who often struggle with the complex language of the textbook. It helps students support their reading comprehension when they do read the textbook and their prior knowledge will be activated as they make sense of the textbook.

Content ELD

A newer term that has surfaced is Content ELD. Content ELD continues to focus on the development of English with clear language objectives, but it is taught within a content area. As opposed to teaching English simply through language arts-based programs, ELD is taught concurrently with content. In Content ELD, language and content objectives are both the focus of every lesson. A Content ELD approach supports English language learners by providing a meaningful context within which students can develop English. "The content area provides meaning contexts for authentic communication as learners collaborate to complete carefully designed academic tasks" (Wright 2010, 46). In addition, I have found that teachers enjoy using strong content such as science or social studies for Content ELD for two primary reasons: (1) content is rich, authentic, and easily accessible to students for real-world connections that enhance comprehension; (2) teachers are able to maximize their instructional time by combining ELD with content instruction.

Content ELD is the time set aside for ELD. It has intentional, explicit language objectives and many opportunities for students to use English orally and in writing. It is also the core time for content instruction. Content ELD can become your science or social studies time of day as well; therefore, it must also contain clear content and measurable objectives with ample opportunities to explore, understand, and make meaning from content.

In order for Content ELD to be successful, teachers must think about the role of language throughout a lesson. The language and content must balance each other out in order for students to excel academically and acquire Content ELD. Figure 6.3 below demonstrates this representation.

Fig. 6.3 Content ELD

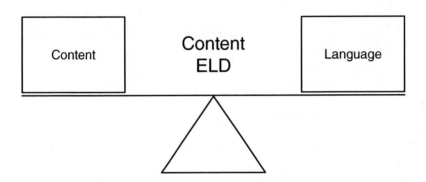

When lesson planning, teachers need to be aware of the content and language they select within the content areas. For example, when creating science ELD lessons, teachers can use an inquiry-based science approach to support strong content knowledge and explicit language development. The table, *Third-Grade Content ELD Lesson,* on the following pages provides an example of how to combine strong content with explicit language instruction.

Third-Grade Content ELD Lesson

Content Objective
Students will be able to identify different types of environments and describe their unique characteristics.

Language Objective
Students will be able to identify and describe a given environment, both orally and in writing.

Lesson Sequence	Teacher Says/Does	Student Says/Does
Engagement	Teacher places pictures of different environments around the room. Underneath each picture is the inquiry T-chart with the following written on the chart: • What do you see? • Questions you have: The teacher pairs students based on their second-language acquisition level and asks them to visit every poster and make a note on each T-chart.	The students will work with partners to complete the inquiry charts around the room. At this stage of the lesson, students will use their own language to explore the content. After all partnerships have commented on every picture, the teacher will give each pair one of the pictures along with its respective inquiry chart to share with the class.
	The teacher models how to share an inquiry chart with the class.	This is the teacher's opportunity to listen in and hear what students already know about the content and the language that they use to talk about it.

Third-Grade Content ELD Lesson *(cont.)*

Lesson Sequence	Teacher Says/Does	Student Says/Does
Instructional Sequence	The teacher reads aloud from the students' textbook about different environments. Every student should have his or her own copy of the text to follow along.	Students follow along as the teacher reads about different environments from their course textbook.
	The teacher asks students to look through their textbooks at the pictures of the environments. Students are instructed to do the following: 1. Use sticky notes to label nouns in the picture. They write one word per sticky note. 2. Use sticky notes to label adjectives for the nouns. They write one word per sticky note and place it next to its noun sticky note. 3. Working with partners, they create three sentences that describe their environment. 4. Students then share their descriptions and the class will try to identify the environment. This is a meaningful opportunity to provide explicit language instruction. The teacher can model and provide sentence frames appropriate for students' ELD levels.	With partners, students use sticky notes to label nouns and adjectives seen in pictures of different environments in their textbook.

Lesson Sequence	Teacher Says/Does	Student Says/Does
Application	A picture of an environment is posted for all students to see. The environment is labeled using key vocabulary from the unit. Students are asked to write in their notebooks a description of the environment.	Students will take their knowledge of the environment (content knowledge) and the language of the description that they were modeled and taught (language development) and write a description.
	Students engage in a Tea Party where they read their descriptions to one another. Refer to the Tea Party strategy (pages 128–129).	To support language fluency, students practice descriptions through the Tea Party. In addition, they practice using content vocabulary as they describe their environment.

The lesson is an example of how teachers can include clear, measurable language and content objectives and explicitly model and facilitate English language development within the content areas. "More recently... the pre-K to 12th grade ESL profession has, at least in theory, become increasingly committed to content-based approaches to language and to describing the kinds of English language proficiencies needed to succeed academically" (Valdes 2010, 111). In practice, I am also seeing more schools and districts turning to Content ELD as a way to contextualize language development and to ensure that students are provided language-rich content instruction.

Academic Language Development and Content ELD

In Chapter 3, we talked at length about academic language and how to facilitate academic language development throughout the curriculum. What is important to discuss here is the difference between Content ELD and ALD. What makes ALD instruction different from Content ELD is the focus on teaching content, while making language development a by-product. Teachers set clear content objectives and intentionally plan for language development.

Critical to ALD is that teachers provide comprehensible input to support students' content knowledge and provide opportunities for guided comprehensible output. Here is where we find carefully planned lessons using SDAIE strategies to support English language learners. SDAIE strategies are used to help make content comprehensible for English language learners. We want to also plan for ELD opportunities where students are able to engage in conversation and interact. These opportunities for language output support students' academic language development. They talk about what they are learning in the content areas. This includes using content vocabulary, and functions and forms of language particular to the content area. We need to provide opportunities for students to use language throughout the curriculum to promote academic language development. This is the language students will need to be successful in their educational careers.

Conclusion

English language learners are exposed to complex language throughout the school day. They need ongoing support to make meaning when they encounter language used for a variety of purposes. Teachers must understand what it means to teach about language and through language. This includes knowledge of ELD, Content ELD, and ALD. A strong understanding of what it means to be explicit about language and provide students with varied, daily opportunities to use language is critical for facilitating high levels of academic language. English language learners need support both to make sense of the content and concepts with which they are presented, and then to be able to share their thinking and learning in English.

Reflection Questions

1. What opportunities do you provide your students for thought, talk, and interaction?

2. What opportunities do you provide for students to practice using newly learned vocabulary orally and in writing?

3. What opportunities do you offer your students to engage in daily discussions on diverse content with different partners?

4. What are some lessons where you included both a language objective and a content objective to promote academic language development?

Concluding Thoughts

Teaching is the profession that prepares the next generation of critical and creative thinkers, inventors, and entrepreneurs—the next leaders in all fields and industries. We are the profession that connects to every profession. I am confident that teachers entered this profession believing in *all* children, including those students that may struggle and create additional challenges for us as teachers. Those days when teachers feel helpless and tired and ready to throw in the towel are the days that remind us that we are teachers. This is the work of teaching. Every day is a challenge. Every day is a success. Every day is a new story to share. And every day we have touched the life of a child.

I want teachers to think optimistically when they are faced with the challenge of working with English language learners— not because they are English language learners, since all learners are presented with challenges, but because too often a deficit perspective exists when talking about the education of English language learners. We need to be re-energized, and inspired to think about English language learners as a dynamic and exciting group of students who give us opportunities to continue to grow and learn as teachers. Each year, every new group of students we teach presents new challenges and new ways of learning. We must start our year ready for the challenge of getting to know our students as learners, as individuals, and as members of diverse communities of English language learners. Do not lose sight of why you became a teacher. Take time to celebrate your profession, and remind yourself that you have been given the gift of teaching. You are a teacher, and with that comes a great deal of responsibility. Make every opportunity a learning opportunity for your students and make amazing use of the time you have with children every day from bell to bell and beyond. I thank you for being a teacher, and I encourage you to consider your struggles as learning opportunities. Successful teaching may be difficult, but because of it, together we become better people.

Appendix A

Cognates

English	Spanish
angular	angular
audience	audiencia
author	autor
battle	batalla
biography	biografía
border	borde
calculate	calcular
calendar	calendario
canal	canal
cannon	cañón
capacity	capacidad
conflict	conflicto
debate	debate
declare	declarar
dialect	dialecto
empire	imperio
enemy	enemigo
fabricate	fabricar
facilitate	facilitar
factor	factor
fascinate	fascinar
globe	globo
glory	gloria

Cognates *(cont.)*

English	Spanish
gradual	gradual
hemisphere	hemisferio
historian	historiador
horizontal	horizontal
imagine	imaginar
justice	justicia
justify	justificar
kilogram	kilogramo
labor	labor
legal	legal
legislator	legislador
liberty	libertad
list	lista
magnitude	magnitud
map	mapa
margin	margen
national	nacional
nationality	nacionalidad
native	nativo
noble	noble
object	objeto
observe	observar
pacific	pacífico
palace	palacio
past	pasado

Cognates *(cont.)*

English	Spanish
quarter	cuarto
ray	rayo
reality	realidad
reason	razonar
rebel	rebelde
reference	referencia
reflect	reflejar
second	segundo
senate	senado
telescope	telescopio
temperature	temperatura
thesis	tesis
traditional	tradicional
tragedy	tragedia
train	tren
tunnel	túnel
ultimate	último
united	unido
velocity	velocidad
verb	verbo
victory	victoria

Cognates

English	German
acute	akut
algebra	algebra
alphabetic	alphabetisch
architect	architekt
athlete	athlet
balcony	balkon
battery	batterie
camel	kamel
candidate	kandidat
cannon	kanone
compass	kompass
complex	komplex
compromise	kompromiss
congress	kongress
curve	kurve
data	daten
decimal	dezimal
electron	elektron
electronic	elektronisch
energy	energie
equator	äquator
era	ära
experiment	experiment
fable	fabel
fabrication	fabrikation

Cognates (cont.)

English	German
fabulous	fabulös
farm	farm
figure	figur
flag	flagge
fossil	fossil
gallon	gallone
gas	gas
general	general
glossary	glossar
helium	helium
hurricane	hurrikan
hypothesis	hypothese
iceberg	eisberg
idea	idee
igloo	iglu
illustrate	illustrieren
insect	insekt
jet	jet
jewel	juwel
journalist	journalist
kilogram	kilogramm
kilometer	kilometer
latin	latein
machine	maschine
magnet	magnet

Cognates *(cont.)*

English	German
massive	massiv
medicine	medizin
method	methode
microscope	mikroskop
million	million
mineral	mineral
monarchy	monarchie
muscle	muskel
music	musik
nature	natur
navigation	navigation
negative	negativ
nitrate	nitrat
nuclear	nuklear
number	nummer
object	objekt
objective	objektiv
ocean	ozean
octagon	oktogon
ozone	ozon
palace	palais
paper	papier
perspective	perspektive
philosophy	philosophie
photograph	fotografie

Cognates *(cont.)*

English	German
planet	planet
plural	plural
profit	profit
project	projekt
quiz	quiz
radius	radius
reaction	reaktion
regular	regulär
revolution	revolution
satellite	satellit
sculpture	skulptur

Appendix B

Language Functions and Forms

Language Functions	Possible Sentence Frames Examples (Forms)	Cue Words	
Agreeing and disagreeing	I agree with…but… I believe…was right when he/she said…but I disagree with…when he/she said… I am in favor of… I think…was wrong when he/she said… I agree with….However…	agree believe think right wrong	but however disagree wrong in favor
Expressing likes and dislikes	I like… I want… I love the way… I enjoy… I don't like… I dislike…	like enjoy love adore want	dislike hate do don't
Identifying	It smells like… It looks like… It feels like… It sounds like… It tastes like…	**Sensory Words:** looks feels sounds	tastes smells
Refusing	I will not… I do not want to… He or she did not want to… I wouldn't… I didn't… I am not going to…	not wouldn't didn't shall not would not did not	won't will not can not am not do not

Language Functions and Forms *(cont.)*

Language Functions	Possible Sentence Frames Examples (Forms)	Cue Words	
Sequencing	First…then…lastly… At the beginning…next…finally… In the beginning…in the middle…at the end… First…second…third…last…	**Ordinal Words:** first second third beginning middle end	finally next then later last(ly)
Wishing and hoping	I wish… If only I… Maybe I can… I hope… If I had…then…	hope wish maybe if…then	want perhaps crave
Comparing	…is…but….is not …has…but…does not …can…However,… …can…whereas…cannot Though…can…cannot	but whereas however can/cannot	is/is not different as opposed to
Classifying	…belongs in this category because… …is part of this group because… I organized the…by… You can group these together because…	belongs part of group order	organize sort together

Language Functions and Forms *(cont.)*

Language Functions	Possible Sentence Frames Examples (Forms)	Cue Words	
Explaining	...is...because... The reason for...is... He or she was....For example... I would like to clarify that...	is/is not because for example	make clear such as clarify
Warning	Don't...because... Be careful not to... Watch out for... Stay away from...because... I warned you not to...	don't be careful watch out caution stay away	inform advise notify alert warn
Hypothesizing	I think...because... I believe...because... Maybe...is...because... Perhaps...is the reason why... It's possible that...	think believe perhaps maybe	assume possible imagine
Planning and predicting	I think...is going to happen because... Perhaps he or she will... Maybe he or she will... because in the text it said...	think believe perhaps maybe	expect guess see coming
Commanding	Begin by... First you will...then... Start by...then...finally... Before you begin...then... I order you to...	start/begin then/finally order demand	command will should do not

Language Functions and Forms *(cont.)*

Language Functions	Possible Sentence Frames Examples (Forms)	Cue Words	
Reporting	It all began when… The incident/event took place… It is/was about… What happened was… The real story it that… It all started because…	tell state describe story details happened report	testify give an account convey inform recount inform event/incident
Expressing	I would just like to say… I find… I was thinking… I just had a thought… I have an idea… I am sure that… I realize now that…	think idea thought find/found sure/unsure	state communicate put across say realize
Obligating	You have to…because… He was forced to…because It was necessary because… You must…or else…	must force necessary	require make mandatory
Evaluating	I would have to disagree with…because… I agree that…but… I think… I decided that… Based on what happened, I believe…	agree disagree decided accept	however further furthermore think

Language Functions and Forms *(cont.)*

Language Functions	Possible Sentence Frames Examples (Forms)	Cue Words	
Expressing position	I support the idea/position that…because… I would agree that… I side with…because… I do not believe that… because… In my opinion…	support agree disagree opinion	view side with position
Expressing obligation	I must… I feel I have to… I believe it is my responsibility to… I should…because…	must obligated should responsibility	duty commitment requirement have to
Inferring	I believe the author is trying to say that… Even though it doesn't say so in the text, I think… The more I think about this passage, I realize… After reading this page, I think that… I suppose the author is trying to say that…	infer believe think thought	assume understand suppose conclude
Suggesting	I would recommend… After listening to/reading…I suggest… I would advise you to… I propose…	propose advise recommend	suggest

Language Functions and Forms *(cont.)*

Language Functions	Possible Sentence Frames Examples (Forms)	Cue Words	
Criticizing	I don't think he or she should…because… I dislike the way… He or she should not have… I disapprove of the way in which… I commend him or her for… I admire how…	disapprove dislike approve praise	admire commend congratulate applaud

Chen and Mora-Flores 2006

Appendix C

Glossary

academic language—the functions, forms, vocabulary, and fluency one needs to demonstrate his or her thinking and learning across the curriculum

Academic Language Development (ALD)—the knowledge, understanding, and use of language particular to an academic context; involves the functions, forms, and vocabulary students use to understand and demonstrate their learning across the curriculum

Basic Interpersonal Communication Skills (BICS)—the language we need to engage in social conversations

cognates—words that are similar in spelling, meaning, and pronunciation from one language to another

Cognitive Academic Language Proficiency (CALP)—the level of language development where students are able to understand concrete and abstract language and express their thinking across the curriculum

Common Underlying Proficiency (CUP) hypothesis—the cognitive/academic proficiency that languages operate through the same central processing system.

comprehensible input—communication that is slightly above the students' level of English ability

comprehensible output—a hypothesis that states that we acquire language by attempting to communicate in newly acquired language but fail and therefore need to try again

Content ELD—focuses on the development of English with clear, language objectives but is taught within a content area.

English Language Development (ELD)—the study and development of the English language including listening, speaking, reading, and writing also known as English as a Second Language (ESL)

English Second Language (ESL)—the study and development of the English language including listening, speaking, reading, and writing also known as English Language Development (ELD)

false cognates—words that look and sound similar and are pronounced similarly from one language to another, but have a different meaning

inquiry charts—taking students from basic recall of information to questioning their thinking and learning by writing down ideas of what they learned or understood and then generating questions

language functions and forms—the reasons why we use language; the language structures we use to communicate within a function of language

language-rich environment—an environment that allows students an opportunity to engage in dialog and discussion; a classroom that is filled with oral and written language for students to hear, see, and practice

morphology—the study of morphemes, the smallest unit of meaning

phonemic awareness—knowledge of the sounds of a language and the ability to manipulate those sounds to produce words

phonics—word study of the sounds of the English language and the letters that represent those sounds; the connection between sounds and symbols that support students ability to decode words

second-language acquisition—the process by which people learn a second language in addition to their native language(s)

Specially Designed Academic Instruction in English (SDAIE)—strategies that help students comprehend content by presenting it through rich contexts that make the learning comprehensible

Structured English Immersion (SEI)—a program model where instruction is delivered only in English but in a way that makes it comprehensible for students learning English

References

Adams, M. J. 1990. *Beginning to read: Thinking and learning about print.* Cambridge, MA: MIT Press.

Anderson, R. C., and W. E. Nagy. 1992. The vocabulary conundrum. *American Educator* (16): 14–18, 44–46.

Bear, D., L. Helman, M. Invernizzi, S. Templeton, and F. Johnstone. 2006. *Words their way with English learners: Word study for spelling, phonics, and vocabulary instruction.* Upper Saddle River, N.J.: Pearson Merrill Prentice Hall.

Beck, I. L., and M. G. McKeown. 1991. Conditions of vocabulary acquisition. In *Handbook of reading research* vol. 2, ed. R. Barr, M. Kamil, P. Mosenthal, and P. D. Pearson 789–814. New York: Longman.

Beck, I. L., M.G. McKeown, and L. Kucan. 2002. *Bringing words to life: Robust vocabulary instruction.* New York, NY: Guilford Press.

———. 2008. *Creating robust vocabulary: Frequently asked questions and extended examples.* New York, NY: Guilford Press.

Boyd, M. P., and D. L. Rubin. 2002. Elaborated student talk in an elementary ESL classroom. *Research in the Teaching of English* 36 (4): 495–530.

Calkins, L. 1994. *The art of teaching writing.* Portsmouth, NH: Heinemann.

Capps, R., M. Fix, J. Murray, J. S. Passel, and S. Herwantoro. 2005. *The new demography of America's schools: Immigration and the No Child Left Behind Act.* Washington, D.C.: The Urban Institute.

Chen, L., and E. Mora-Flores. 2006. *Balanced literacy for English learners, K–2.* Portsmouth, NH: Heinemann.

Collier, V. P. 1987. Age and rate of acquisition of second language for academic purposes. *TESOL Quarterly* 21: 617–641.

Cummins, J. 1980. The construct of language proficiency in bilingual education. In *Georgetown University Round Table on Languages and Linguistics*, ed. J. E. Alatis, Washington DC: Georgetown University Press.

————.1984. Wanted: A theoretical framework for relating language proficiency to academic achievement among bilingual students. In *Language proficiency and academic achievement*, ed. C. Rivera (14–18, 44–46). Clevedon: Multilingual Matters.

Freeman, D. E., and Y. S. Freeman. 2004. *Essential Linguistics: What you need to know to teach reading, ESL, spelling, phonics, and grammar.* Portsmouth, NH: Heinemann.

Gandara, P., and F. Contreras. 2009. *The Latino education crisis: The consequences of failed social policies.* Cambridge, MA: Harvard University Press.

Geva, E. 2006. Second-language oral proficiency and second-language literacy. In *Developing literacy in second-language learners: A report of the national literacy panel on language-minority children and youth*, eds. D. Augusta and T. Shanahan, (123–139). Mahwah, NJ: Lawrence Erlbaum.

Gibbons, P. 1993. *Learning to learn in a second language.* Portsmouth, NH: Heinemann.

————. 2002. *Scaffolding language, scaffolding learning.* Portsmouth, NH: Heinemann.

————.2009. *English learners, academic literacy, and thinking: Learning in the challenge zone.* Portsmouth, NH: Heinemann.

Girard, V., and P. Spycher. 2007. Deconstructing language for English Learners. *Aiming High.* Sonoma County Office of Education.

————. 2010. Reading instruction for English language learners. In *Handbook of reading research*, eds. M. Kamil, E. Moje, and P. Afflrebach Newark, DE: International Reading Association.

Goldenberg, C. 2010. Reading instruction for English language learners. In *Handbook of reading research*, ed. M. Kamil, P.D. Pearson, E. Moje, and P. Afflerback, 1–55. Newark: International Reading Association

————. 2008 (Summer). Teaching English language learners: What the research does—and does not—say. *American Educator* 32 (1): 8–23, 42–44.

Greene, J. P. 1998. A meta-analysis of the effectiveness of bilingual education. Sponsored by The Tomas Rivera Policy Institute; The Public Policy Clinic of the Department of Government, University of Texas at Austin; The Program on Education Policy and Governance at Harvard University.

Haggard, M. R. 1982. The vocabulary self-collection strategy: An active approach to word learning. *Journal of Reading* 26 (3): 203–207.

Hearne, D. 2000. *Teaching second language learners with learning disabilities*. Oceanside, CA: Academic Communication Associates.

Kadic, M. and M.A. Lesiak. 2003. Early reading and scientifically-based research—National Title I Directors' Conference. http://www.2ed.gov/admins/lead/read/ereadingsbr03/edlite-index.html.

Krashen, S. 1985. *The input hypothesis: Issues and implications*. London: Longman.

————. 2004. *The Power of reading*. 2nd ed. Portsmouth, NH: Heinemann.

Krashen, S., and T.D. Terrell. 1983. *The natural approach: Language acquisition in the classroom*. London: Prentice Hall England.

Lesaux, N.K., and M. J. Kieffer. 2010. Exploring sources of reading comprehension difficulties among language minority learners and their classmates in early adolescents. *American Educational Research Journal* 47 (3): 596–632.

Lucas, T., A. M. Villegas, and M. Freedson-Gonzalez. 2008. Linguistically responsive teacher education: Preparing classroom teachers to teach English language learners. *Journal of Teacher Education* 59 (4): 361–373.

Moats, L. C. 2000. *Speech to print: Language essentials for teachers.* Baltimore, MD: Paul H. Brookes Publishing.

National Literacy Panel. 2000. Report of the National Reading Panel—Teaching children to read: An evidence-based assessment of the scientific research literacy on reading and its implications for reading instruction (report of the subgroups). Washington, DC: National Institute of Child Health and Human Development.

Office of English Language Acquisition (OELA). 2007. *The Growing number of limited English proficient students 1995–96–2005–2006.* Washington, D.C.: Office of English Language Acquisition

Robinson, F. P. 1960. *Effective Study.* 3rd edition. New York: Harper and Brothers.

Sarmiento, L., D. Beltran, and E. Mora-Flores. 2010 (Fall). Integrating science and ELD: A curriculum model for English learners. *Leadership Magazine.* A publication of the Association of California School Administrators.

———.2010. Thinking and doing approach to language development: Science and ELD. Paper Presented at the CALSA First Annual Research to Practice Conclave, UCLA. http://www.calsa.org

Saunders, W., and G. O'Brien. 2006. Oral language. In *Educating English Language Learners* In F. Genessee, K. Lindholm-Leary, eds. W. Saunders, and D. Christian. (14–63). Cambridge, NY: University Press.

Scarcella, R. 2003. *Accelerating academic English: A focus on the English learner.* Oakland, CA: Regents of the University of California.

Schafersman, S. D. 1991. An introduction to critical thinking. http://critical thinking.org (accessed November 14, 2010).

Stabb, C. 1986. What happened to the sixth graders: Are elementary students losing their need to forecast and to reason? *Reading Psychology* 7(4): 289–96.

Stanovich, K. E. 1986. Matthew effects in reading: Some consequences of individual differences in the acquisition of literacy. *Reading Research Quarterly* 21: 360–406.

Valdes, G. 2010. Between support and marginalisation: The development of academic language in linguistic minority children. *International Journal of Bilingual Education and Bilingualism* 7(2): 102–132.

Willig, A. 1985. A meta-analysis of selected studies on the effectiveness of bilingual education. *Review of Educational Research* 55:269–316.

Wittgenstein, L. 1953. *Philosophical Investigations.* Translated by G.E.M. Anscombe. New York: The MacMillan Company

Wright, W.E. 2010. *Foundations for teaching English language learners, research, theory, policy and practice*, Caslon Publishing: Philadelphia.

Notes

Notes

Notes